WORLD WAR II REVISITED–

*Memoirs of a
Forced African Conscript*

WORLD WAR II REVISITED–

Memoirs of a
Forced African Conscript

Robert Peprah-Gyamfi

Perseverance Books

WORLD WAR II REVISISTED–
Memoirs of a Forced African Conscript
This is the first part of a duology – the prequel of *TWINS DIVIDED.*

Published by Perseverance Books
Divine Favour Enterprises Ltd
Loughborough,
LE11 2FB

www: peprah-gyamfi.com
Email: divinefavour@peprah-gyamfi.com

Cover design and book illustration by Isaac Kofi Quansah.
Cover photo: British Army Generals on a visit to West African troops in Burma (Source: Imperial War Museum K9290).

ISBN: 978-0-9955524-2-5

"Those who would judge us merely by the heights we have achieved would do well to remember the depths from which we started."

Dr Kwame Nkrumah, 1st President, Republic of Ghana

Table of Contents

~~~

Acknowledgement

M any, many thanks to my wife Rita, who maintained order in the home whilst I was locked up for hours on end in my study trying to put my thoughts together; and our children Karen, David and Jonathan for bearing with my frequent absence.

Enormous thanks to my editor Dr Charles Muller, proprietor of Diadem Books, for the graceful editing and the splendid foreword.

Foreword

~~~~~~

D r Peprah-Gyamfi has written a history book with a difference! It tells the story of two identical twins living in a small rural town in the Gold Coast who set out, one bright Sunday, on a hunting expedition. The reader is so easily drawn into what is at first a delightful and charming story about two innocent and adventurous boys who set out with a friend to bag something for the pot – but then something frightening and very unexpected happens to the two of them, and for years the twin boys are separated.

In the main, the story follows the lot of the younger twin, Kakra, and in the process the reader almost unwittingly gains a vast amount of knowledge and insight into the history of the Second World War on two fronts – in what was Italian East Africa and Burma. Speaking for myself, the revelations are unexpected and enormously instructional, especially if you have an interest in the role played by countries in West Africa in the war years prior to the independence of Ghana and other African countries. The role played, and the sacrifices made, by recruits from West Africa, including countries such as Nigeria, Sierra Leone and Ghana, were unquestionably significant, as this book will reveal. The irony is that their role and their sacrifices were not truly appreciated at the time, perhaps even made light of in recent years, because of the prejudices of the pre-war colonial masters towards Africans at the time. This story, seen largely through the eyes of an African partisan, Kakra, puts the record straight! It is ironic, too – in fact, shocking – that these brave recruits, many who gave their lives for King and Empire, were not even recruits – but young boys who were forcefully abducted to form part of the fighting force in the front lines of battle!

The author has not written a dry and clinical history book full of dates and facts. Instead, he has resuscitated the past by making it alive, seen through the eyes largely of Kakra and other participants. We share their endurance, their fortitude, as they face hunger, exhaustion, carry equipment on their heads and shoulders through rainforests and jungles, create air strips for planes with sheer muscle power, face bullets on the battlefield and, in quieter moments, discuss and argue about the meaning of it all. We also share their friendships, their camaraderie, as well as the frustrations of these conquering heroes (those who have survived) as they wait for long tedious months for a troopship to take them back home to West Africa, to be reunited with their loved ones.

This is not just a history book, but a human story – one that has taught me much about human endurance and the worth of human beings, whatever their colour and creed.

Charles Muller
MA (Wales), PhD (Lond), DEd (SA), DLitt (UFS)
Marbella
16 June 2017

PART 1
FORCED CONSCRIPTION

Chapter 1
The ill-fated hunting expedition

—ᴟᴟᴟᴟ—

IT WAS LATE AFTERNOON on Sunday December 3, 1939. The sun, the faithful and trustworthy friend of the residents of Kojokrom, was making its final rounds of the day in the blue skies high above the little settlement.

As was usually the case on almost every day of the year, the sun's journey through the tropical skies had begun around 6 o'clock in the morning. Around midday, it had assumed a position in the sky almost perpendicular to that of the little town. The sky was clear, blue and deprived of clouds, leading the community directly exposed to the intense heat emanating from its heavenly host. Everyone felt the heat and sought shelter under the roofs of the homes or under the shades of large trees.

After about three hours of a scorching midday heat, temperatures began to drop a few degrees. The villagers had still about three hours to get things done before the final departure of their daily heavenly visitor would plunge the little settlement into deep darkness. Devoid of electricity, they would have to resort to traditional-style kerosene-powered miners' lanterns and Swiss kerosene lamps to find their way in the dark.

Familiar with the short transitional time between the departure of the sun in the skies and the arrival of darkness, which on nights deprived of moonlight could be so thick as to seem almost palpable, creating the impression of the surrounding world being draped in a blanket of darkness, the three teenagers on a hunting expedition decided to call off their hunt and return home before the onset of darkness.

Though neither Attah Panin nor his identical twin brother Attah Kakra, nor Nyamekye their friend, possessed a watch, they had learnt, just like most others in the community, to use their shadows to estimate the time of day. In the morning, their shadows were long and to their left; at midday they assumed a short stature beneath them; towards the evening they became elongated again, but this time to the right side of their bodies.

The hunting expedition had been undertaken in spite of the disapproval of Asoh, the mother of the twins.

"Let's go hunting for Gambian pouched rats!" Nyamekye had come up with the idea as the three were out playing the night before. Nyamekye, though still a teenager, could well be described as a seasoned hunter. With the two dogs of his parents as his aid, he seized any opportune moment to go out hunting, targeting in particular Gambian pouched rats and grass cutters, all of which abounded in the thick tropical forest that surrounded the town.

"It's not a bad idea!" Kakra concurred. "We could give part of the catch to our parents and sell what is left and keep the money for ourselves!"

"Kakra and money; always coming up with plans to make money!" Panin retorted.

"My good brother, the reality is that without money you are nothing!"

"That does not mean we should spend all our time thinking about it!"

"You don't have to strive for it with the main intention of keeping it for yourself", his junior brother countered, adding, "But there is nothing wrong in seeking it for yourself and using part to help others in need!"

"This is no time for a philosophical reflection on the matter of money, Panin and Kakra", Nyamekye cut in. "Are you joining me in the venture, yes or no?"

"Joining you!" the twin brothers replied as if with a single voice.

"Okay then, see you tomorrow! Are you coming with your dog?"

"He is good for nothing, our Big Ben!" Kakra laughed. "He cannot even catch a mouse!"

"Okay, then you can leave him to relax at home. I will come with our two dogs. They are really well versed in the business."

Not long after that, they left for their respective homes.

As Panin and Kakra headed home, they knew their decision to accompany Nyamekye the next day wouldn't go well with their parents, especially Asoh, their mother. The devoted Catholic that she was, she would almost certainly explode with fury at their decision to go hunting on a Sunday instead of accompanying her to church. Their father, Duku, wouldn't be a problem. Though he was also a Catholic and attended church just as regularly as his wife, he was not as devoted.

It was his habit to visit the palm wine tappers' hut, a drinking spot in the village, to enjoy one or two calabashes of palm wine – a white-coloured alcoholic drink obtained by tapping the sap of the oil palm tree.

On his return home, his behaviour often led Asoh to suspect his mind had, even if temporarily, been taken over by alcohol, and she would confront him with these words:

"It is not a good Christian practice to drink!"

"Madam, did you not hear the passage read in church recently, I mean the one concerning Jesus turning water into wine?"

"That's no licence to drink!"

"Drink, but not to get drunk!"

"But you appear drunk already."

"Who is drunk?"

"I can smell alcohol on your breath!"

"In whose breath?"

"Yours!"

"It's probably from my hands; I had to hold the calabash to drink from it!"

"You better be careful, my dear! That is how it all began with my uncle. 'Drink, but don't get drunk!' he used to tell everyone who cautioned him about his excessive drinking habit. In the end he lost control over his drinking. At that stage, everyone was calling him 'oweeye!' (the Alcohol Addicted!). He kept on drinking until his belly became swollen, just like that of a heavily pregnant woman. One day he collapsed and died on the spot!"

Duku always sought a good opportunity to end the discourse with his other half before it turned into what he termed a never-ending *moral lecture*.

Indeed, he had been married to the woman he had in the meantime nicknamed "the Parrot" long enough to realise that unless he gave in on such occasions, she would continue to squawk on and on like a parrot – till who knew when?

On rising the next morning, instead of heading for the riverside to fetch water to wash in preparation for attending church, Panin and Kakra put on the worn-out khaki-coloured pair of shorts and blue T-shirts they usually wore when joining their parents for work on the farm.

On seeing her boys clothed in this manner, Asoh immediately questioned them.

"What is the matter with you boys? No one is going to the farm today, so why put on these shabby clothes?"

"Going hunting!" Kakra replied boldly.

"Going what!?" Asoh inquired, not believing her ears.

"We're going hunting – going after rats, grass cutters, squirrels!" Kakra stated emphatically. Though the younger of the two, he had virtually assumed the role of spokesperson for the pair, ahead of his more reserved senior brother.

"You are going *nowhere*!" Asoh stated unequivocally, her anger clearly written on her face.

"Please!" both brothers pleaded.

"No; not on a Sunday!"

"Please give us this last chance!" Kakra persisted. "We hope to make a good catch. We shall donate half of whatever we get to the family and sell the rest for our pocket money."

"No!"

"Please!"

"No!"

"What's the matter?" inquired Duku, who had just returned home from a visit to the community male latrine at the outskirts of the little settlement.

"They are going hunting on a Sunday instead of attending church!"

"Leave them alone, Asoh! My boys are of age, so leave them to decide for themselves!"

"*You*, Duku!" Asoh replied, exasperated. "You must teach your children to serve the Lord!"

"But that is exactly what they do every day, my two decent, loving and polite boys – they let their light shine!"

"Going in search of rabbits and rodents on a Sunday, instead of going to church is not a good way of letting one's light shine in the world!"

"I believe in practical Christianity rather than in Christian formalities. As far as I am concerned, one does not have to attend church every Sunday to be a good Christian. Have you forgotten the Bible passage read at church last Sunday... 'The Sabbath was made for man and not man for the Sabbath'!"

"Enough of that, Duku! You're always quoting Bible verses to excuse the shortcomings in your Christian walk!" Asoh burst out, hardly able to hide her fury with the three *male gang members* of the family, as she sometimes called them whenever they stood together against her.

As might be expected, Panin and Kakra were delighted by the intervention of their father and stood firm in their decision to join Nyamekye in the hunting expedition. Asoh, on her part, realising there was little she could do to dissuade them from their plans, kept quiet.

Shortly after breakfast Nyamekye, accompanied by his two hunting dogs, *Poor No Friend* and *Jack Tiger,* came to call his two friends.

"Take good care of yourselves, boys", Duku advised them as they set out. "Don't wait till it turns dark before returning home!"

"Don't forget to pray for us Mama", Panin said, turning to Asoh.

"I will. This is going to be the last Sunday you are going on a hunting expedition instead of attending church – okay?"

"Well noted!" her boys replied in one voice.

As already indicated, the expedition was aimed in particular at grass-cutters, Gambian pouched rats and squirrels.

The grass-cutter, also known as the greater cane rat, belongs to a small family of African rodents. They can grow to about two feet in length in the longest individuals and attain a weight of about 20 pounds.

The grass-cutter has rounded ears, a short nose, and coarse, bristly hair. They feed on grasses and cane; they also have a taste for cultivated foods, in particular maize and sugar cane. They were quite common in that area, inhabiting the thickets of the thick vegetation.

Also known as African giant pouched rats, the Gambian pouched rats on their part usually dwell in hillocks and termite mounds. They hide in their homes during the day and at night venture out under the cover of darkness to look for food – which is made up in the main of vegetables, insects, palm fruits, etc.

The hunting expedition turned out to be a wearisome venture with a meagre outcome. On a few occasions the intrepid hunters, assisted by their dogs, had given chase to grass-cutters hidden in the thick undergrowth. On all such occasions, the rodents virtually vanished into thin air before they could catch up with them.

The boys had had little luck with the Gambian pouched rats as well.

On about half a dozen different occasions much effort was expended to provoke them to come out of their respective hideouts in the mounds, only for them to escape before their eyes.

It was long after midday, just as they were about to call it quits and return home, when they managed to obtain the only "hunting trophy" of the day – not without great effort.

On their arrival at a particular hillock every sign gave evidence of its occupation – fresh claw marks left in passages and alleys leading into the heart of the hillock or mound.

To get the rat out of its hiding place, they cut off a long stalk from the surrounding bush, inserted it into one of the openings and moved it to and fro in an attempt to disturb the peace of the occupant and by so doing force it into the open. Despite all their efforts, the occupant appeared unimpressed. Initially, they thought of giving up and returning home.

"No, let's give it a last try", Nyamekye urged. "I just hate the idea of returning home empty-handed after all our efforts!"

So they embarked on the next stage, to stuff the openings into the hillock with dried leaves that had fallen from plants growing in the area, and then set them alight, in the hope of getting the occupant to come out of its hiding rather than get suffocated by the smoke. To get the smoke into the heart of the hillock, they used a makeshift fan woven from the branches of a nearby oil palm tree. That did the trick! Minutes later the poor beast emerged from one of the openings.

Poor No Friend who was guarding that opening, showed no mercy at all. Pouncing on the animal, it grabbed it by the neck and mercilessly bit it to death.

With at least *one trophy* in their hand, they called off the expedition and embarked on the walk back home. The expedition for the day was conducted mainly in a huge tropical rain forest that bordered the little town. Because they had penetrated so deep into the vegetation, they were about one and half kilometres away from home. They would have to walk about three hundred metres along a bush path in the heart of the forest before joining a rough, rugged road that vehicles scarcely frequented, that led to Kojokrom.

As they learnt from their parents, in former times the only way residents of Kojokrom and the neighbouring villages and hamlets could reach Oseikrom, the comparatively large town located on the trunk road leading to Kumasi, was by way of a bush path similar to the one they were treading.

Residents of the area did not only have to walk the distance of approximately five kilometres to Oseikrom to catch the next available vehicle to their various destinations, they also had to carry their dried cocoa beans ready for sale, on their heads, to the purchasing agents at Oseikrom. From there, further transportation would be required to reach the port at Takoradi.

As the production of cocoa beans, a good source of foreign exchange for the colony, increased, the colonial administration, probably on grounds of economics rather than love for the population, decided to extend the road from Oseikrom to Kojokrom.

The road in the meantime did not only facilitate the transportation of cocoa; it also facilitated the carting of tropical timber, abundant in the thick forest of the area, for further transportation to the port at Takoradi for export to far distant lands.

But for the trucks that turned up occasionally to cart timber and cocoa beans, the road was less frequently travelled. Indeed, days, sometimes weeks, went by without any vehicle turning up at Kojokrom, leaving residents who had something to do at Oseikrom and beyond little choice other than to undertake the journey to Oseikrom on foot.

Just about a hundred metres before the bush path joined the main road, Panin, who was walking behind the group, all of a sudden called out:

"Keep on going, boys! I'll catch up with you in a moment."

"What's the matter?" Kakra inquired.

"I said, keep going!"

"What's the matter?" Kakra persisted.

"Typical Kakra!" Nyamekye remarked. "As always, poking his nose into Panin's affairs!"

"That's exactly what he also does to me", Kakra said in defence.

"I have to obey the call of nature! Are you satisfied, *Mister* Kakra?"

"Yes, I am, my dear. Take good care of yourself!"

"I will; see you soon."

So saying, Panin made for the woods.

Just as they stepped on the main road from the bush path, Kakra and Nyamekye saw a military truck on the road, heading towards Kojokrom. It pulled to a stop on reaching them. There was a passenger beside the driver in the front compartment. Pretending they wanted to ask them the way, they beckoned the boys to come near to the front cabin.

"Is this the way leading to Kojokrom?" the driver inquired as the two approached.

"Yes indeed, we are also heading for that village", Nyamekye replied.

Just at that moment two men in military uniform, each holding a gun, sprang out of the back of the vehicle and charged up to the boys, pointing the guns at them.

"Stand still, or else we shoot you!" one of them shouted at them.

"Climb into the vehicle!" the second man ordered them.

"Please, please!" both begged in unison.

"Hurry up and get on board if you wish to live!"

They hesitated a moment to follow the instructions, which caused the men to kick them violently, their military boots inflicting pain on their poor victims.

"Adjeyiii! Adjeyiii!! Adjeyiii!!" Kakra and Nyamekye shouted at the top of their voices, as if with a single voice, putting up as much resistance as they dared. Their words were in *Twi* (*Twi* being the language spoken by the Akan ethnic group) and expressed their distress and fright. "Adjeyiii! Adjeyiii!! Adjeyiii!!" they repeated the agonising cry a few times.

Meanwhile the dogs had begun to bark loudly.

"Get on board, boys!" one of the men shouted. "I'm counting up to 10. On the count of 10, I'll blow your brains out of your stupid heads if you are not in the vehicle!"

Sensing the seriousness of the situation, Nyamekye decided to give up any resistance and follow the instructions of their captors; he beckoned Kakra to do likewise.

Hardly had they climbed into the back of the vehicle when the driver set it in motion. Instead of heading in the direction of Kojokrom, it quickly turned and headed back in the direction from which it had come.

* * *

Panin had initial difficulty pressing the waste out of his bowels. He seemed to be constipated, quite unusual for him. After pressing and pressing for a few minutes, he was done with it. Soon he was back on the path the others were treading. He hurried to catch up with them.

Just as he was about 20 metres away from the road he was heading towards, he suddenly heard the loud screaming and yelling of the other two.

"Adjeyiii! Adjeyiii!! Adjeyiii!!" – accompanied by the loud and fierce barking of the dogs.

Panin ran towards the scene as fast as his legs could carry him, wondering what the hell was going on.

As he approached the scene, he could also hear the loud noise of an engine as well as the screeching of tyres – akin to that of a vehicle attempting to speed away.

Panin reached the road just in time to see the last traces of a dark green truck as it disappeared around a bend in the road, leaving behind it a trail of dust, the two dogs in hot pursuit. To his utter consternation, Kakra and Nyamekye were nowhere to be seen!!

Was it out of desperation, was it because he seemed momentarily to have lost his mind, that Panin pursued the vehicle with all the strength he could muster, calling on the top of his voice the names of Kakra and Nyamekye as he gave chase?

After running wildly after the vehicle for several hundred metres, the reality of the situation began to dawn on him – the two had been forcefully abducted. For several minutes, he cried uncontrollably! For a while he thought he was in a dream – a nightmare for that matter. Kojokrom was a serene, peaceful little town; but for the rough, bumpy, little-used road ending at its very centre, it may well be described as a minute spot at the end of the world – literally cut off from the rest of the world. That such an isolated location could be the scene of such a spectacular abduction was beyond his comprehension. He wondered who was behind the forceful seizure.

There had been rumours of people going about in search of human body parts to be used in rituals. The rumours had it that such criminals pounced on their innocent victims in isolated locations, killed them in cold blood, took their body apart, removed the parts they needed for their rituals and either buried what was left of the bodies in hastily dug shallow graves or left them to the mercy of the elements.

Such seizures were purported to happen in the most isolated places. The perpetrators were said to resort to the method of ambushing. Hiding in the bush in pairs or in small groups, they were said to pounce on victims who happened to be passing by alone.

That was, however, a far cry from what he had just witnessed – a truck being used to forcefully seize two individuals they had come across by chance, reverse direction and speed away with their victims to "only God knows where" was incomprehensible to him.

Dazed, confused, unable to control his tears, almost paralysed by his emotions, he finally decided to head for home. The sun was setting; it would soon turn dark, so he had to hurry.

*   *   *

Meanwhile the truck in which Kakra and Nyamekye had been abducted was speeding away, shaking violently as it sped along the rugged, pothole-ridden road.

The scene that met their eyes on climbing into the truck left them with little doubt as to the seriousness of the situation they found themselves in. Lying on mats spread on the floor of the vehicle, blindfolded and handcuffed, were three other captives, one of them about Kakra's age, the other two about 10 years older. Keeping a close watch over them was a third soldier, also armed.

Kakra and Nyamekye were immediately blindfolded, handcuffed and ordered to lie on the floor, just like the other three, by the two soldiers who had been directly involved in their abduction.

After travelling a considerable distance over a stretch of road which, judging by the way the vehicle kept on shaking all the time they travelled, had a rough and bumpy surface, the vehicle suddenly pulled to a halt.

Kakra wondered what the matter was.

"Anyone wanting to obey the call of nature?" one of three men guarding them inquired in the Twi language.

Was he aware not everyone in the vehicle was conversant with the Twi language? Perhaps he was, for he repeated the instruction in a language that sounded like Hausa, a language spoken mostly in the north of the colony, and which was Latin in the ears of Kakra.

That was exactly what each of the captives had waited for, for each of them responded in the affirmative.

"You will be offered the opportunity to do so, one after the other", the soldier said. "My colleague will escort you whilst I keep watch over the rest of you. Woe betide anyone who attempts to escape!" he warned, "That individual can count today his last day on earth! Has the message sunk in?" He addressed them first in Twi, then in the strange language already referred to.

"Yes", Kakra responded meekly.

The four remaining did likewise.

As the first captive was led away, Kakra took advantage of the situation to put forward further demands.

"I do not only have the urge to open my bladder, I also feel thirsty and hungry!" he stated,

"Hungry and thirsty!" one of the officers who seemed to be the leader of the group howled at him. "We don't have anything on board for you. You have to wait until we get to our destination."

It took several minutes for each of the five captives to have the opportunity to empty his bladder, and in two cases to open the bowels as well.

Finally, after a break lasting about half an hour, the journey was resumed.

* * *

Panin in the meantime continued his difficult walk home.

As he walked on, accompanied by the two dogs, he remained very attentive, flinching at any sound that bore the least semblance to that of the engine of an approaching vehicle, and so he quickly made for the woods; but, as he had expected, no vehicle passed by during the rest of his walk home.

When he was several metres away from home, he was spotted by his sister Tawiah, who was two years his junior. On seeing him, she ran to meet him.

"Where are the rest?" she inquired immediately she caught up with him.

For a while Panin kept his silence.

"Tell me Panin – where is Kakra? Where is your friend Nyamekye?"

Panin wanted to wait until he reached home before breaking the news, but the persistence of his younger sister soon became unbearable to him.

"They are gone!"

"Where?"

"Gone!"

"Where?"

"They have taken them away!"

"Who?"

"They drove them away in a vehicle!"

"Who drove them away?"

"I don't know! They drove them away! They are gone!" Panin could no longer hold back his tears and began to weep bitterly.

Tawiah ran ahead of him towards their home. Soon she got to the compound of their home. Still panting for breath, she began:

"Mama, Papa!" she began, panting for breath.

"What's the matter?" Asoh inquired.

"Panin is returning home alone, Kakra and Nyamekye are not with him!"

"Where has he left them?" Asoh questioned, her heart beginning to race within her chest.

"I also wanted to know. In reply, he could only say that 'they have taken them away!'"

"Who has taken them away?" Asoh cried at the top of her voice.

"I don't know. You can find out from him yourself!"

Asoh could hardly bear it any longer! With her whole body shaking uncontrollably, she handed Nana Yaw, the barely nine-month-old boy she was breastfeeding, to Tawiah, sprang on her feet and ran to meet Panin, who in the meantime was a few metres away from the perimeters of their compound.

"Panin, where is Kakra? Where is Nyamekye?" she demanded.

"Please allow me to get home to tell my story."

"No, I can't wait. For God's sake, Panin, tell me what has happened."

"You wait a minute, I am almost at home. I want to narrate it in the presence of everyone."

"Lord, please; Lord, please; Lord, please have mercy!" Asoh screamed at the top of her voice as she moved helter-skelter around Panin.

On seeing Asoh's state of excitement and the tears in Panin's eyes as he caught up with them on the perimeters of their home, as he was on his way back home from a visit to a friend, it was clear to Duku that something was seriously amiss.

"What's the matter?" he inquired.

"Please wait a moment. I will tell you everything on getting home", Panin replied with a broken voice.

Soon the whole family was gathered around Panin.

Hardly able to control his tears, Panin narrated in detail what had happened. Though not displaying the same emotions as his wife, Duku was nevertheless just as shocked to hear what Panin had to say.

The news of the disappearance of the two spread like wildfire through the little town. Soon almost the whole population of the settlement descended on their home to express their sympathy and show their solidarity.

It took the family a while to digest the news of the disappearance of Kakra and his friend.

After the initial shock came the thought of what to do next. In line with tradition, any resident of a community was required to keep the chief of the community informed of any unusual happenings in the settlement, even if the traditional leader by whatever means, happened to have got wind of the matter.

In line with tradition, Duku hurried to the *Ahenfie*, as the residence of the chief or king of a community is known in Twi, to inform him about the disappearance of Kakra and Nyamekye.

The chief, who happened to be Asoh's nephew, on hearing what Duku had to report, called an emergency meeting of the town's traditional committee that very night. Though based on Panin's account they gave themselves little chance of finding them; still, the committee decided to organise a search party first thing the next morning, to comb the area in question, if per chance they could discover the abducted boys, dead or alive.

*   *   *

After they had driven for several hours – over a period that felt like an eternity to Kakra – the vehicle finally pulled to a stop. Still blindfolded, they were ordered to get out of the vehicle. Though none of the captives wore a wristwatch, from the conversation of their captives, Kakra realised it was a few minutes past midnight.

Moments after the vehicle had pulled to a stop, the blindfolds covering their eyes were removed by their captors – not so the handcuffs. Still closely guarded, they were ordered to alight from the vehicle. Next, they were marched into a small room and given something to eat and drink.

Finally, they were each handed a pillow, a mat and a sheet of cotton to serve as body cover and led into a large hall. Already sleeping on mats spread on the floor were several others – Kakra estimated there were about 50 of them. Though some were still awake, most were deeply asleep.

The five new arrivals were instructed to spread their mats in one corner of the hall which remained unoccupied. Bone-tired and experiencing general bodily aching from the arduous journey, Kakra was soon overcome by sleep.

Chapter 2
The blood of the disloyal and fearful soldier for the bayonet!

—*mm*—

T he next day after a breakfast of *koko* (porridge made of corn meal) and bread, the men who had all arrived over the weekend were led into a hall, which was several times smaller than the one serving as their sleeping quarters, to be addressed by an important personage, as part of their induction.

After they had taken their seats on hard rows of wooden benches, the officer who introduced himself as Commander Cobra arrived to address them.

Was it a way of instilling fear into his men? Perhaps, for instead of addressing them in a friendly and decent manner, he began by shouting at them.

"Everyone, listen to me! My name is Commander Cobra! You need to respect me; otherwise you will see red. Indeed, just as a single bite from the cobra can lead to death, anyone of you who chooses to disobey Commander Cobra can reckon with a deadly bite from him, okay, men!"

There was an eerie silence from the timid recruits.

"Have you got the message, men?!"

The eerie silence in the hall prevailed.

"On the count of three each one of you should shout, 'Yes, Commander Cobra!' Okay?"

There was still absolute silence in the room. The faces of the men betrayed their anxiety.

"One. two, three!"

"Yes, Commander Cobra!" the assembled men yelled from deep down their throats.

A short silence followed.

At that juncture, Kakra decided to gather all the courage he could muster to ask a question that burned in his heart.

"Commander Cobra, may I please ask a question?"

"Shut up, young man!" Commander Cobra screamed at him. "You don't talk unless I ask you to do so, okay!"

Deep silence prevailed in the hall.

After a short while, Commander Cobra continued:

"Various rumours have been circulated concerning the reasons why you are here. Some of the rumours have it that you are being sold into slavery. What a fabrication! Men, the slave trade ended several years ago. No one is selling you to slave masters. We must however be on our guard because indeed there is a threat of enslavement hanging over the heads of each man or woman endowed with a black skin colour.

"Adolf Hitler does not only harbour the crazy idea of conquering the whole world, he also has plans to exterminate anyone who does not fulfil his own set of criteria for those who deserve to populate this world – Blacks, Jews, Roma people, etc.

"As a first step towards the achievement of his demonic ambition, he launched an attack on Poland. The war in the meantime has spread not only to the whole of Europe but also to Asia and North and East Africa.

"The Empire needs soldiers to fight to resist the diabolic schemes of Nazi Germany. You are going to be part of that force!"

Though Kakra had in the meantime been told by a couple of those who had been in the camp about the likely involvement of the men in the Second World War efforts of the Empire, he had refused to believe it. The message delivered now to his ears by a commissioned officer left no more room for disbelief.

The shock of the revelation coupled with the poor ventilation of the overcrowded room would soon prove too much for him to bear. He began to feel as if the world around him was spinning in circles before his eyes. Before long his legs could hardly carry him. Moments later his knees buckled and he collapsed onto the floor.

"That's a sign of cowardice!" Captain Cobra remarked in an unsympathetic tone. "Men, get him out of the room and into the open – he needs some fresh air."

Nyamekye and three others carried him out of the hall.

The officer appeared to have had second thoughts on the matter, for he interrupted his speech and went out to find out about the unwell recruit.

"Are you alright?" he inquired when he got to where they had placed him.

The fresh air indeed was what Kakra required, for moments after his exposure to the fresh air outside, he regained his strength.

"Thanks, I am fine", he replied.

After staying outside for a few minutes, Kakra felt much better and returned to the hall.

On seeing him, the officer who had interrupted his speech to give Kakra time to recover, resumed his address.

"We are not going to send you to the battlefield unprepared. Over the next several weeks, we will put you under intense military training to prepare you for the challenging task ahead. The plan is to give you at least 12 weeks' basic military training.

"Indeed, there is an urgent need to prepare you adequately for the assignment ahead!

"My understanding is that, almost every new recruit we take on has never in his life worn a pair of sandals, let alone a pair of boots! How can one expect to send such raw *stuff* to the battlefield!" He burst into laughter on saying that. He continued:

"I also hear that apart from a few of you who hail from the coast, the great majority of you are unable to swim!

"My goodness, what a raw bunch of men I have to deal with! In normal times, most of you present here would be fortunate if you were considered for menial jobs in the army. Well, these are not normal times. The Empire is at war, not only on one front, but on several. So, His Majesty has placed you under my care and expects me to weld you into a mighty and robust fighting force in the service of King and Empire!!"

He paused for a while. Then continued:

"Well, I will do my best; yes indeed, I will put my best foot forward to mould you into hard-core soldiers capable of handling the worst of enemies. Take it from me, at the end of your training exercise you will become not only soldiers, you will become a mighty fighting force which every enemy, from north, south east or west of the globe, will learn to fear and respect.

"I don't know how long the training will last. We do indeed live in unsettled times. Everything indeed will depend on the turn of events on the battlefield.

"Should the war turn and go terribly against the Empire in the next several days, we may have to shorten the training period and move you to the battlefield earlier than planned."

After about 45 minutes of a monologue from Commander Cobra on matters relating to their impending training and subsequent dispatch to the battlefield in faraway lands, he finished his speech.

Soon he was on his way out of the room.

Kakra thought the event was over. But no, as it turned out, the speech of the commissioned officer was only the first of several events planned for the day. As he was later told, the occasion was the beginning of the induction week into the Gold Coast Division of the Royal West African Frontier Force, which apart from the Gold Coast boasted troops from the Gambia, Sierra Leone and Nigeria.

No sooner had Commander Cobra left the scene than another soldier, this time an African, mounted the stage.

"May I have your attention, men. My name is Sergeant Adjetey. I am the non-commissioned officer, NCO for short, in charge of operations in this base. Our honoured Commander was here to welcome you. Now you need to be officially registered into the Army. To facilitate the process, we are going to form three groups. This is how we are going to proceed. Starting from the gentleman on the right, we are going to count 1, 2, 3. Then 1,2, 3, and so on. All those in Group 1 will follow Corporal Dogo Moro; Group 2 will be assigned to Sgt Baba Yara whilst those in group 3 will be taken care of by Sgt Komey. So 1, 2, 3... on we go..."

About five minutes of some turbulence followed as the group formation took place. Finally, the process was completed. Group 1 was asked to remain in the hall, whilst the remaining two groups headed for two adjacent rooms.

Though the meeting had so far been conducted solely in the English language, the authorities were aware of the fact that as in the case of Kakra hardly any of the recruits was well versed in the English language. They therefore provided translators for the main languages of the territory – *Ga, Hausa* and *Twi*.

Details were taken of the names, dates of birth (hardly any recruit had their births registered, so ages were estimated and corresponding dates of births assigned), the names of their places of birth or residency as well as the names of two next of kin.

Next a nurse took each man's weight, height and blood pressure.

Finally, the men were clinically examined by a military doctor.

Kakra later found out that some of the new recruits were rejected because they failed to meet the minimum standards set by the Army. These included those who were below a minimum height set by the Army, those who were markedly impaired in vision and hearing as well as those displaying non-healing ulcers. Those who were rejected on the grounds of height were maintained and employed in support roles.

One of those rejected happened to be one of the captives on their vehicle on that fateful day. As it turned out he displayed a visual impairment which made him unfit not only to be enlisted for a combat role but also for support services. How much Kakra had hoped he too would be deemed unfit to be recruited and allowed to go back home! As it turned out, this was wishful thinking on his part!

The registration process took the whole morning to complete. Before dismissing them for lunch, Sgt Dogo Moro urged the new recruits to join an assembly at 2 p.m. in the same place for what he described as a very vital part of the registration procedure – the swearing of the oath.

"Every recruit is required to swear an oath of allegiance or attestation to the King and Empire. Recruits may choose to swear on the Bible or the Koran. Those not wishing to swear on either of the two books may choose to swear on either the bayonet or an effigy of their fetish or a talisman or whatever they deem appropriate."

A fellow recruit of Kakra's Gold Coast Division
swearing on the bayonet
(Source: Imperial War Museum WA 13)

As instructed, the recruits returned to the designated location after lunch.

Kakra chose to swear on the Bible. With the sacred Christian Book pressed to his forehead, he swore allegiance to King and Empire.

Muslim recruits swore on the Koran. Kakra was struck by the fact that about two-thirds of those taking part in the swearing ceremony that day happened to be Muslims.

Recruits who swore on the bayonet held it up high before them, kissed it and recited: "If I am disloyal or show fear in battle, let this bayonet drink my blood."

The swearing ceremony ended the day's activities.

After the registration and swearing ceremony, each of the recruits was handed a set of military clothing – uniform, singlet, underwear, sandals and military boots as well as a set of cutlery.

Thus ended the first full day of Kakra's new life as a military conscript.

Chapter 3
The reassuring revelations of a sympathetic officer

~mm~

B ack at Kojokrom, at the dawn of the new day, with Panin, the key witness in the matter leading the way, the search party left as planned in search of the two missing boys. Though not bound by law, each healthy man in the community aged about 20 and beyond, and strong and healthy enough to do so, was expected to participate in such a communal undertaking. In the end, almost every male person strong enough to do so joined in the search.

On their arrival, the search party began a systematic combing of the area. From time to time one of them called aloud the names of the missing boys, in the hope, even if faint, of getting a response – but to no avail as it turned out. After spending the whole day searching in vain for signs of life of the missing duo, the search was finally called off just before the onset of darkness.

Prior to the establishment of the colonial administration, the chief would have been the highest authority in the matter. With the arrival of the Europeans that was no longer the case. They were then expected to report the matter to the police without delay – easier said than done! The nearest police station was at the district capital, Kofikrom, about 30 kilometres away. They had to walk to Oseikrom to join a vehicle to travel about 25 kilometres, not eastwards towards Kumasi, the Asante capital, but rather in the opposite direction.

That night Duku approached the local clerk of the cocoa-purchasing agency to collect a loan against cocoa beans he had just began drying in the sun. It would require about 14 days of exposure to sunlight to get them dry enough to be sold.

As for Duku, cocoa was the main cash crop not only for the farmers of Kojokrom, but also for the majority of those dwelling in central and southern parts of the Gold Coast endowed with a tropical rain forest.

The next day, Tuesday, Duku and Panin left home at dawn to embark on their journey to the police station. After walking the distance to Oseikrom, they waited about an hour to catch a vehicle heading for Kofikrom. Finally, they reached the police station shortly before midday.

After waiting at the reception for about half an hour they were invited into one of their rooms. There were three police officers present. Each of them was seated behind a table busily occupied with something.

On their entering, a well-built female officer aged about 40 asked them to take their seat in front of her desk.

"How can I help you, sir?" she began, addressing Duku.

"We have come to report an incident", Duku began. "I will allow my son Panin to do the talking. Indeed, he was the sole eyewitness of the happenings."

"Okay, go ahead, young man", the officer addressed Panin.

Hardly able to maintain his composure Panin recounted the events of the fateful day to the police.

At the end of his narration, the interrogating officer read back to them what had been recorded. Since Panin had not attained the age of adulthood, Duku was required to sign for him. Since Duku on his part could not read and write, he attested his approval with a thumbprint. In all it took the officer about an hour to complete the interview.

After bidding the officer goodbye, they left the interview room and made their way along the open compound towards the gate of the police station.

Just as they were a few metres away from the exit gate of the police compound they heard someone behind them shouting, "Father, father!"

They turned to look. They saw one of the two other police officers who were in the room during the interview hurrying towards them.

"Father, wait a minute."

The two did as requested. Soon he caught up with them.

"I want to confide something in you", he began in a low voice. "What I am about to reveal is not official. Please promise to keep it to yourself, okay?"

"You have my word", Duku assured him.

"You villagers seem not to have any idea of what is presently going on in the world?"

"What is the matter?"

"Have you not heard about the war raging in Aburokyire?"

"What war?"

"The war started by Adolf Hitler!"

"Adolf *Who*?"

"Hitler!"

"Who is Hitler?"

"He is the leader of Jaaman Aburokyire. He has initiated a war in Aburokyire, which in the meantime has engulfed several other countries in Aburokyire."

"But I thought Aburokyire is one and the same country!"

"No, father, that is not the case. Just as we are made up of various tribes – Akans, Gas, Ewes, Dagartis, Hausas, etc., they are also made of different ethnic groups – Enyiresi, Jamaan, Italian, French, etc."

"Well, I am not aware of that!"

"Of course, I did not expect an uneducated peasant like yourself to be informed about such matters. In any case, that is what is happening in our world. As we speak, fierce battles are being fought between Jamman-Buroni and their allies on one side and Enyiresi-Buroni and their allies on the other."

"But what has that got to do with the disappearance of my son and his friend?!"

"Well we are a colony of Enyiresi-Buroni. My understanding is that the war seems to be going against our colonial masters. In their desperation to avert possible defeat, they are recruiting able-bodied men from their colonies worldwide to assist them in their war efforts."

"Still, I don't get the connection between what you are saying and the disappearance of the two boys!"

At that stage, the officer turned round to make sure no one else was around them. Speaking almost in a whisper, he continued:

"It appears our colonial masters are not getting enough men to sign up voluntarily to fight for them so they have resorted to forceful recruitment!"

"That cannot be true! Why should they send others to war against their will?"

"Please, please, don't say it loud! In particular don't tell anyone I revealed this to you! Indeed that is what is going on. Our chiefs, yes including very prominent ones, whose names I will not mention, are colluding with the foreigners! Not for nothing! I am told they are paid substantial sums for each suitable recruit they deliver. The practice is for the paramount chiefs to instruct their sub chiefs to look for suitable recruits; they then dispatch vehicles to collect them.

"Soldiers have also been dispatched to the countryside to look out for candidates suitable for recruitment. When they spot such individuals in an isolated location, they pull up beside them, capture them at gun point, and hurriedly drive them away.

"I am fully convinced a similar fate has befallen your relatives! Certainly, that is not a consolation, but at least you can be almost certain that they have not been victims of ritual murderers going around killing people for the sake of their body parts.

"As your son stated in his report, he saw a green truck speeding away – with all certainty it was a military truck.

"The forceful recruitment is happening everywhere. To avoid possible capture most men in the countryside leave home at dawn and hide in the bush only to return home under the cover of darkness. The result is that these days when one travels through villages, one only meets women, children and the elderly. You only have to pray for a speedy end of the war and, in particular, that the two manage to survive the conflict."

"Thank you very much for this information. I can only hope that Kakra and Nyamekye – if indeed they have been forcefully recruited – are able to survive the ordeal and return home one day alive."

"Well, father, I wish you all the best. Stay strong and do not give up hope – never!"

Saying that, he patted the shoulders of both and headed back to his office.

After waiting at a designated station for a while, they finally caught a vehicle back to Oseikrom. It was late in the evening when they got to Oseikrom.

Just as they had done in the morning, they had to walk the distance to their final destination on foot. Everyone, apart from Asoh, who had decided to keep wake until their return, were deep asleep at the time they got home.

Asoh received the news they carried with a mixed feeling – whilst still mourning over the disappearance of Kakra, the revelation by the police officer ignited a ray of hope in her, indeed hope, though minute, that one day she might see her beloved Kakra again.

Chapter 4
The mischievous twins of Kojokrom and their teacher friend

—*mm*—

N ot only Panin was devastated by the disappearance of his soulmate; everyone else in the settlement was also.

Over the next several days, a thick cloud of sorrow descended on the community; a feeling of collective grief was everywhere evident.

After about two weeks of what can be described as a collective state of communal melancholy, life gradually began to return to normalcy for most of the residents.

Not so in the case of Panin; over the next several days, weeks, even months – he remained inconsolable. He just could not come to terms with the disappearance of his Kakra, indeed his very soulmate. It appeared as if part of his flesh had been severed from him to the extent that he was no longer his complete self.

He hardly ate or drank anything. Even if he had the desire to eat, the sight of food made him nauseous.

By nature, both he and Kakra were slimly built individuals. After several days of almost complete food deprivation, his body literally became a pack of bones!

It was heart-breaking not only for his parents and close family members, but for the whole community at large to watch him waste away!

Just as Panin sorrowed over the sudden departure of his soulmate, Kakra could also hardly bear the fact of their separation! Panin and Kakra were, simply put, body and soul. Let us go back to a time preceding the birth of the twins to appreciate this.

Hardly had Duku performed the traditional marriage rites in respect of his attractive young wife and taken her home than the villagers noticed a change in her features, pointing to a possible pregnancy. In time, the fact that she was expecting a child became obvious to the outside world.

The pregnancy coming so close on the heels of the marriage set the rumour mill of the community ablaze. Some gossips had it that the two had been sleeping together contrary to the traditional requirements which expected couples to refrain from intimacy until after the performance of the marriage rite. Some rumours even had it that she became impregnated by someone else long before she got married to Duku!

While dismissing the rumours as baseless, Duku himself was startled at the speed at which the belly of his beloved was expanding. With the only health post in the area located at Kofikrom, no pregnant woman in the village, mainly for reasons of finance (the token fee demanded amounted to a fortune for the impoverished community) and convenience (for reasons already known to the reader), attended antenatal care.

The unusual pace at which her abdomen expanded led not only the pair but several others to suspect she was perhaps carrying more than one child.

About three weeks prior to Duku's own estimated delivery date, she got up one day to notice she was steadily losing fluid. Soon she began to experience pain. In time, the pain increased in intensity to the point of becoming almost unbearable.

"Hurry and fetch Nana Akosua Aba!" Nana Asieduah, Duku's mother who had been called to the scene, instructed one of her grandchildren.

Nana Akosua Aba, what a personality she was! Through her own personal experience delivering her six children at home with the assistance of traditional midwives, and also observing other relatives deliver their children, she gradually gained experience in the area of childbirth. In due course, she began to function as a traditional midwife in the village. She had in the meantime developed into a traditional birth assistant, respected not only in her community, but in the surrounding villages.

She was kind-hearted and dedicated to her patients; she not only provided her services for free but also reserved one room in her extended family home for women who arrived from outside the village to solicit her help.

Fortunately, she had not as yet left for work on her farm when the little boy dispatched to fetch her turned up. On hearing what the little lad panting for breath from his quick run had to tell her, she wasted no time in hurrying to the aid of the labouring young woman.

It turned out to be a protracted labour which challenged the skills of the veteran midwife. Just at the point when she was considering asking the relative to make plans to rush the woman to the clinic at Kofikrom (which would have involved carrying her on a makeshift stretcher to Oseikrom to catch a vehicle to their final destination), the head of the baby emerged in the birth canal. Minutes later, to the joy and relief of all present (apart from the two directly involved, Nana Asieduah and Maame Mansa, Asoh's mother, were also present) a bouncing baby boy was delivered.

Just as they awaited the delivery of the afterbirth, Asoh declared to the astonishment of all present:

"I can still feel movement in my body!"

"Are you sure, my dear?" Nana Akosua Aba inquired, tenderly wiping the drops of sweat that had gathered on her forehead. It was just past midday on a sunny day; it was scorching hot and the heat in the little room where the dramatic events were unfolding was hardly bearable.

Asoh's baby – babies as it turned out to be – could not have chosen a worse possible moment, at least from the perspective of their mother, for their arrival on planet Earth.

"Yes, Mama, I certainly think there is another baby down there!" Asoh replied, the intense pain she was undergoing clearly evident in her facial expression.

On hearing that, Nana Akosua Aba knelt down beside her and placed her palm on her belly.

"Please be quiet", she urged everyone present. Devoid of any instruments to assist her in her trade, she had come to rely on her senses in her job.

After about half a minute of feeling the movement in the body of Asoh with her palm, a broad smile passed on her lips.

"Yes indeed, I can confirm that there is at least one other baby on the way!"

A mixed feeling of joy and tense expectation filled the room.

The four women witnessing the events unfolding had to wait a bit, though, for the expected baby seemed in no hurry to emerge from its "hideout". Almost half an hour after the delivery of his brother, during which time the experienced traditional midwife performed one manoeuvres after the other, aimed, as she told those tensely watching her, at facilitating a quick birth, the second child, also a boy, was finally delivered.

To ensure there was no other baby left in Asoh's womb, Nana Akosua Abah went on her knees again beside the new mother and urged the rest to be quiet.

"No third child, please! I have had enough!" Asoh cried out in response.

"Well, let me check, my daughter!" Nana Akosua Abah replied.

After placing her hands on the stomach and on the woman's lower abdomen and feeling it attentively for a while, she got up from her knees.

"Any further baby to be expected?" Nana Asieduah inquired.

"No; definitely not", came her reply.

Not long after the birth of the second twin, the afterbirth was also delivered.

Giving birth to twins was a rarity in the little town; indeed, none of those present, not even the very aged, could remember the last time twins and, for that matter, identical twins were born there.

Oral tradition had it that very, very long ago before that day, one of Duku's ancestors had given birth to twin girls. As they grew up, the two were so temperamental and mischievous, that they were taken to be witches! That led the extended family to seek ways and means to get rid of them. The opportunity came when one day slave dealers arrived in the village. On hearing the news, leading members of the family held a secret meeting and devised a plan to sell them into slavery. Aware that their mother would be strictly against the idea, they concocted a plan and lured the twin girls to a secret location without their mother's knowledge where the deal was executed. The slave owners are reported to have sold them on to European slave dealers who in turn shipped them away to a very distant land never to return to the village!

Their mother, on hearing about the scheme of the extended family, became so heart-broken she decided to end her life through hanging. It was a family secret rarely told. Duku wondered, had the twins possibly decided to return to the world in a different gender?

In line with tradition, there was a naming ceremony on the eighth day. Usually, parents have the tendency to name their first child after the paternal grandparents – a son after the grandfather; a daughter after the grandmother. The rules are not rigid though.

Duku did not hesitate a second in deciding to name them after his father Kwasi Amaniampong. In the end they were known respectively as Kofi Amaniampon Attah Panin and Kofi Amaniapon Attah Kakra – Kofi, by virtue of being born on a Friday, Attah by virtue of their being twins, Panin for senior; Kakra for junior.

Whereas identical twins are generally known to share several things in common, the close bond between Panin and Kakra went beyond the ordinary.

Somehow the physiological functioning of their respective bodies seemed also to be in tune with each other – be it the feeling of hunger, be it the feeling of thirst, or the urge to open the bowels, or the urge to empty the bladders. You may go on naming them – but the moment one of them felt the need to engage in such an activity, the other followed suit! The fact that the two were the only identical twins not only in Kojokrom, but also the surrounding villages, made them the pride not only of their community but also of those bordering on their own.

Hardly anyone in the community sent their children to school in those days. Several factors accounted for that. There was no law requiring parents to send their children to school. With no compulsion on them to do so, parents preferred to keep their children, who usually offered assistance to their work on the farms, at home rather than send them to school.

Also important was the issue of money. Parents had to pay for the education of their children. Even if it could be regarded by the wealthy as a token fee, it amounted to a great deal for the predominantly poor peasant community.

Even if Duku and Asoh had the means to take their boys to school, the difficulty of accessibility proved a stumbling block. There was no school in the little town. The nearest facility was at the district capital, Kofikrom. They would have to find a resident there who was prepared to permit them to stay over during the week for lessons and return home at the weekend. Such an individual was not forthcoming.

Despite the above obstacles, Duku and Asoh were nevertheless determined to offer their children education. They soon realised to their disappointment that their meagre means was enough only to cater for one of the two boys. How do they explain that to two individuals who were almost inseparable?

One day when the boys were about six years old, Duku called them to a quiet place and began:

"We very much want to send you to school. We are facing two problems, however. In the first place, we are struggling to find someone at Kofikrom willing to permit you to stay at their home during the week to enable you to attend lessons. We have not given up yet. I have spoken to our pastor. He is trying to get someone in the church to accept you.

"But even if we find someone, our resources can only pay for one of you. In other words, one of you has to sacrifice for the other."

"No, no, *no*! We are going nowhere – either you send both of us or neither of us!" they replied as if with one voice.

"You have to understand our situation; we just don't have the means to support both of you at the same time."

"Don't worry. In that case, both of us will stay away from school and help you in the fields."

Thus, in the end, the twins stayed away from school.

As they were growing up, Panin and Kakra were not free from mischief. They took advantage of their physical resemblance to outwit not only their parents and relatives but also friends and society at large. One of them would commit some mischief or misdemeanour, only for the other to own up to it.

They looked so much alike even their parents had difficulty differentiating one from the other. They sought to distinguish them by giving them clothes of different colours. Initially the boys protested. When their parents remained adamant, they found a way of outwitting them in their own way – by regularly interchanging the clothes among themselves.

One day as Kakra was peeling an orange with a kitchen knife he accidentally dropped it. It fell on his left foot, inflicting a wound on the heel. It healed, leaving a scar.

Duku and Asoh sought to use the mark to help set them apart. Whenever they sought to do so for whatever reasons, they attempted to draw close to them to have a closer look at the left foot. Discerning their thoughts, the boys took to their heels and denied the investigator the only real tool to help set them apart.

As they reached the age of adolescence the deep bond between them was a source of displeasure to the girls of their age group, who made advances towards the charming looking guys. Instead of the expected reciprocity, the young women were usually snubbed.

There was also something peculiar about them concerning their interaction with members of the opposite sex. On the very rare occasions that they paid particular attention to the advances of a particular girl, to the point of developing some interest in her, it turned out that, curiously, both fell in love with the same individual in question.

Once when they were alone with Asoh, Kakra turned to her and began:

"Mama, we want to ask you a question."

"Go ahead!"

Instead of putting the question, both began to laugh uncontrollably!

"What's the matter with you?" Asoh inquired.

Instead of replying both continued to laugh at the top of their voices.

"Well, if you have nothing to ask, then please leave me alone!"

"No, we have a question", Kakra stated.

"Then go ahead!"

"It's Panin who asked me to find out from you!" Kakra alleged.

"That's not true! It's Kakra himself who first came up with the idea."

"No, that is not true."

"Boys, I have to go to the market to get some dry fish for the family, so if you are not ready with your question, please leave me in peace."

"Well, we want to ask you... Is it permitted for both of us to marry the same woman?" Kakra let the cat out of the bag.

"My Goodness! How did you conceive such a thought! That is unheard of! I don't know whether that is allowed somewhere. As far as we Asantes are concerned, it is a taboo!"

"Then we may well never marry", Kakra asserted.

"Don't say that, my boy. When the time comes we shall look for a suitable woman for you."

"No thanks, we are able to look out for our own wives!" Panin joined in.

For reasons already touched upon, Kakra and Panin stayed out of school. Not so their close friend Ofori. His father was quite wealthy, having inherited considerable property from a deceased relative. It was Ofori who helped Kakra and Panin acquire basic skills in reading and writing. During the weekends, whenever their time permitted, they met either in his home or theirs to be taught by him.

Not only did Ofori teach them to read and write through the knowledge he had acquired in school, he eventually helped them figure out their exact date of birth – which had not been recorded by their illiterate parents.

Ofori was taught in school about the influenza pandemic that swept through the world in 1918–1919.

Duku on his part had the events of the cataclysmic period and gruesome deaths associated with it deeply engraved in his memory, not only by dint of having lost his father and one of his brothers to the deadly disease, but also because of the dreadful suffering he had to endure as a victim of the terrible plague. Fortunately, just at the time when everyone seemed to have anticipated the worst, he unexpectedly turned the corner.

No one recorded the exact date that Kofi Obeng, Duku's father, passed away. One fact remained undisputed among his relatives though – the fact that the sad event occurred on Holy Thursday 1919.

Unaware of the fact that unlike Christmas, which falls on a fixed day in December, Easter falls on different dates of the calendar, Duku had made it a custom to mark the anniversary of his father's demise on each Maundy or Holy Thursday.

It was exactly around midday on the Good Friday marking the third anniversary of the passing away of his father Kofi Obeng that Asoh gave birth to their two bouncing twin babies.

Uneducated as they were, it never occurred to them to at least get one of the few educated residents of the community to record their date of birth. Nevertheless, the information just mentioned was enough to help their playmate figure out their exact date of birth.

The third anniversary of their late grandfather's death would take place in 1922. Though he could not lay hands on a calendar for 1922 to figure out when Good Friday fell in that particular year, with the help of his class teacher he figured out that Good Friday 1922 fell on April 14.

Panin and Kakra were delighted to have discovered their dates of birth. Based on Ofori's figure, they were a little over 11 years old at the time they found out.

Having in the meantime, thanks to Ofori, learnt the skill of writing the alphabet and numerals, they picked up a charcoal stick and boldly wrote their date of birth, 14/04/1922 on one of the walls of their home.

Now each of them had to learn to cope with the absence of the other.

Chapter 5
A futile search for an escape route

~~~~~~~~

Whereas Panin, by virtue of his circumstances, could perhaps afford the luxury of time to brood over the absence of his soulmate, Kakra, on his part, did not have that privilege. While wholly detesting the fact of his captivity, it soon occurred to him that his best recourse was to adapt quickly to the situation if only to survive. This realisation came forcibly home to him on recognition that it was hardly possible to escape from the camp. Indeed, initially he considered that option.

In this regard, he took a walk around the base to figure out whether there could be a chance of sneaking out – but he soon realised to his dismay that it was hardly possible. The whole encampment was secured by barbed-wire fencing, which rose to a considerable height above the ground. There was only a single entrance within the fencing – the main entrance to the barracks – and this was guarded around the clock by heavily armed servicemen.

Even assuming he managed to escape, how could Kakra make it back to Kojokrom? The base was in an isolated place, far removed from any settlement. Apart from a jeep track that led there, there was no normal vehicular road in the vicinity. Some of his mates had told him the jeep track joined a road about seven kilometres away. From there one had to drive approximately 30 kilometres to get to the next town. A further drive of about 15 kilometres led to the capital, Accra. How could he, in case of an escape, make it over the substantial distance to Accra to join a vehicle to Kumasi – travel on foot? Even assuming he made it in such a manner to Accra, how could he reach Kumasi without money?

Probably as a strategy to prevent anyone deserting, none of the new recruits was given pocket money. His understanding was that it was only after serving for more than three months that new conscripts were given some weekly stipends – and that amounted to almost nothing.

With no money in his pocket, how could he make it from Accra to Kumasi and finally to Kojokrom? Taking all these factors into consideration, Kakra decided to give up any thoughts of planning an escape. Instead, he resolved to play by the rules, until a favourable time came when he could return to his beloved village. And if he should die in the army without making it back home? Well, then that would be the end of the matter!

Chapter 6
A raw recruit and a mocking mentor

~mm~

As Kakra soon realised, just as in his case, a great deal of the conscripts, whether they were there voluntarily or involuntarily, had come from the rural areas and were unfamiliar with matters like the wearing of shoes, the use of the toothbrush, the use of the cutlery etc.

To teach the raw recruits how to go about with such matters, mature soldiers were designated to mentor them. Concerning walking in boots, Kakra initially struggled to maintain a proper gait when wearing them; to his delight it did not take long for him to feel comfortable walking in them.

As his mentor taught him the use of the cutlery, he did not stop passing derogatory comments about the "raw recruit from the jungle" who was incapable of handling the dining sets.

Riding in a vehicle was also new to Kakra. Though he had heard his mother narrating instances in his childhood when she took him and his brother on trips in fully packed trucks to visit the district hospital, he had no recollection of those journeys.

Thus, up to the day of his abduction and the ensuing ride in the military truck, he could not recall ever before travelling in a vehicle.

Chapter 7
Dubious recruiting methods and tactics exposed

—mm—

ONE DAY, about a week into their forced conscription, Kakra and Nyamekye were sitting under one of the many trees in the camp when a group of other recruits, three in number, approached them.

"You look quite unhappy", one of them inquired. "What's the matter with you?" "How can I be happy after being torn apart from my family in such a brutal manner?" Kakra said.

"What do you mean?"

Kakra then revealed the circumstances of his and Nyamekye's abduction. "I miss, in particular, Panin, my twin brother!"

"You have got to get over it and make the best out of a bad situation, my friends. Though we were not abducted at gunpoint as in your case, our individual stories are not very dissimilar from yours."

"We have told you our names and how we got here – how did you get here?" Nyamekye joined in the conversation.

"Well, I will begin with myself. I am Nii Odarmetey!"

"A Ga man?" Kakra inquired.

"Yes indeed."

"Who taught you to speak Twi?"

"Well, my father went to Akyem Abuakwa to engage in farming – Begoro, to be precise. I was born in Bukom in Accra but grew up in Begoro. According to my parents, I was a few months old at the time we moved to Begoro.

"My father has four strong boys, I am the third.

"To expand his farm, my father contacted the chief for additional land.

"'You have to offer one of your children in return', the traditional leader told him.

"'In what way?' my father inquired, somewhat confused.

"'To the army, to fight for King and Empire. You have heard about the big war going on and the conscription exercise underway in the whole of the Gold Coast, haven't you?'

"'Yes, one of my cousins who visited from Accra recently spoke about it. No problem, you can have one of my four boys', my father conceded.

"One morning, at dawn, just before we got out of bed, there was a knock on the door of the room where I and my three other brothers were sleeping.

"'Nii, come out", my father called out.

"'Put on your clothes and follow these gentlemen.' He pointed to two solidly built men, each aged about 40, standing nearby. I obeyed without question.

"'We are travelling to Koforidua to pick up something for your father', one of them told me.

"When we got to the main road, a vehicle was already waiting for us. Seated in the back cabin were about half a dozen other young men of about my age. Instead of heading for Koforidua we ended up here.

"Yaw, now it is your turn", Nii addressed his friend on his immediate right.

"I am Yaw Bonsu, from Kyebi. You may as well use the title 'Nana' to address me. Indeed, I am a royal, from the Kyebi Royal family. My uncle who happens to be a sub-chief of Kyebi just picked me up and handed me to the conscription team that had made their weekly call in our area to pick up the weekly quota of recruits demanded of our traditional area."

"Why did he single you out?" Kakra asked. "Surely there were other young men in your family apart from yourself?"

"Good question! I suggest you ask the leading members of my extended family."

"But you must have a clue as to why?"

"Well, they regarded me as being hot-headed, a kind of outcast – not their idea of one who met the traditional expectations of a royal!"

"Do you consider yourself hot-headed?"

"Of course not! You know the mind-set of our people. The younger ones are not expected to contradict the elderly. But I am by nature outspoken. I won't allow anyone to place what I consider to be undue restrictions on my freedom to say what is on my mind. That has led to my present predicament – I was accused by leading members of my extended family of arrogance and disrespect. What I was not aware of was that they had been plotting behind my back to be rid of me! So, the recruitment drive was the opportunity they sought to get me out of the way. In the end, I was tricked into this situation. A group including a white man called on my uncle.

"'They are looking for a houseboy for the white man', my uncle said. 'Go with them to Accra and take up the position.' That is how I ended up here!"

"That is really harsh!" Nyamekye remarked on hearing the story.

"My name is Kofi Awartey", another said. "I am a Krobo. I was not recruited from Krobo territory though, but from an Akan area, namely, Akim Oda. My only fault was that I happened to have fallen in love with the daughter of the paramount chief of the area.

"On several occasions, I was sternly warned to refrain from 'defiling' a royal person.

"Following repeated warnings, I sought to end the relationship. Much as I advised my lover – Yaa Yaa is her name – not to approach me, she did just that!

"One morning, two attendants of the eminent chief called on me.

"'Nana has asked me to summon you to the palace', I was told.

"'What is the matter?' I asked. I was really scared.

"'Don't be afraid', one of the attendants said. 'I have been told to let you know that after much consideration, Nana is now inclined to give up his resistance to your friendship and accept you as his potential future son-in-law. For that to happen, however, he wants to meet you to clarify one or two issues concerning your background. Of course, you don't expect one of our royals to be married to an individual with a questionable background, do you?'

"You are all aware that when a traditional leader calls, his subjects have no choice but to obey the call, so I followed the messenger to Nana.

43

What I was not aware of, shortly prior to my arrival the conscription truck had arrived to collect the conscripts quota assigned to the King for that week.

"On my arrival, I was greeted in an unexpectedly friendly manner by Nana. After the initial greetings, he began:

"'Just as I sent the messenger to call you, these gentlemen arrived.' He pointed to two gentlemen standing a few centimetres away from where we were. 'I have hired their truck –they are going to purchase cement at Pokuase. They do not know the way, so please accompany them and direct them.'

"Not suspecting any foul play, I did as requested. Instead of heading for Pokuase, they took the road to Accra. That is how I ended up here!"

In the end, the five of them became close friends.

In due course Kakra learnt from other recruits that they too had not signed up voluntarily, but rather had been tricked into the situation by their traditional leaders. The traditional leaders employed several methods to achieve their goal. Only two methods are cited below:

In one instance, they had been invited to an assembly before the traditional leader for an important announcement. As they gathered there, a truck pulled by. They were asked to join it to collect something for the chief. Instead of heading for the stated location, they were driven to a recruitment centre.

In another case, they had assembled to perform some form of communal labour. As they were at work to perform an activity for the benefit of the community – constructing a public latrine, building a school block, weeding around their respective settlements, etc. – a truck pulled up near them. A dozen or so strong men were told to get on board. They were told they were being driven to a site to collect construction material – sand, stone, cement, etc. Instead of heading for the supposed collecting site, they were driven to a conscription centre.

Chapter 8
A heartbroken twin struggling to adjust to military life

‒‒‒‒‒‒‒

KAKRA had to get used to the regimented daily routine of a soldier as against the free-going, unregulated, even lacklustre lifestyle of a village dweller.

Whereas in the village he could adopt a laissez-faire attitude to life, he soon realised that in the army he needed to adjust quickly to a strictly disciplined and highly organised lifestyle characterised by a strict adherence to a set of military rules.

The daily routine began with the blowing of the bugle, a brass instrument like a small trumpet. That was the signal for everyone to get out of bed. Woe betide he who overslept! That individual or individuals, as the case may be, would surely have to reckon with the whip in the hands of a superior officer sent around the large sleeping hall to enforce compliance.

At the latest by 6 o'clock, everyone was expected to be present on the parade ground for the early morning exercise session, which went on till 8 o'clock, followed by an hour's breakfast break.

Yet more sets of military training and exercises – running, marching, drilling, as well as instructions in the use of the rifle, the bayonet, the grenade and other military equipment and instruments – followed breakfast.

There was a short period of rest after lunch before the servicemen were called upon again to undergo still more training – drilling, marching, jogging, bayonet drilling, rifle firing, etc. After the tough, demanding and bone-breaking training regime of the day, the recruits, really worn out, retired for the night.

Concerning the training in the use of weapons–their basic weapon was a bayonet-fitted rifle. The basic training in its use involved initially bayonet drill. The practice involved charging at an imaginary enemy – a sandbag swinging from a rope on a wooden frame – with the bayonet held out in front.

Other bayonet drilling lessons involved sparring with other soldiers in how to use it in various battlefield conditions. The next stage in the training involved training in the use of the rifle itself.

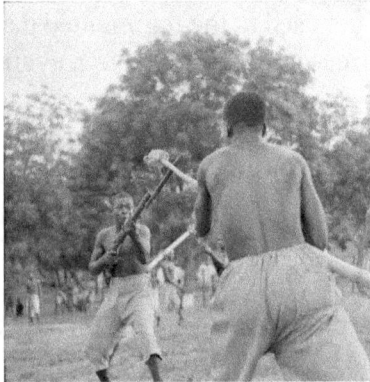

Kakra and other Gold Coast recruits
undergoing bayonet drilling exercise
(Source: Imperial War Museum WA 252)

Kakra's fellow recruits undergoing rifle training
(Source: Imperial War Museum WA 373)

As Kakra learnt from his white instructors, the rifle carried the name of the Bren Gun and was manufactured in the European city of Brno in a country whose name sounded like Latin in the ears of the raw recruit from the Asante heartland, namely Czechoslovakia. It had a rapid rate of fire, removable barrel, and weighed scarcely over 10 kilograms.

Talk of the training in the use of weapons! The idea of having to point a gun at others, yes shoot, and perhaps kill others, troubled Kakra greatly. But how could a soldier about to be deployed in conflict ever avoid such a scenario?

How he wished he would never find himself in that situation! But it was too late. He would have to put his principles aside. It was a matter of survival. It was not his choice to be in the army in the first place. Circumstances – or was it fate or destiny? – had forced him into the situation. He would have to find a way of confronting the enemy and come to terms with his conscience.

Unless of course he chose, deliberately, to end it all – indeed, to resign himself to his fate and intentionally expose himself to the enemy, in a manner as to offer the opponent the opportunity to shoot and kill him.

Indeed, during the first several days of his forced conscription, he seriously considered ending his life, either directly through his own doing, or by placing himself carelessly in harm's way.

47

In time, however, the dark clouds that descended on him in the immediate aftermath of his abduction began gradually to dissipate. Instead of resigning himself to fate, he resolved instead not to give up without a fight. Yes, he would do whatever was in his power to stay alive, indeed, to survive the conflict – for however long it might take.

As Kakra later found it, the Bren Gun was widely employed in the Second World War. It was his companion, not only during the East Africa campaign, but also in his engagements in Burma. With it, he had not only to fight for King and Empire, but also to defend his own skin.

How many enemy soldiers came to harm, indeed lost their lives, as a result of his direct use of his "companion in war", he could not say. He did not even want to consider it; it was war, and war is a terrible thing. As previously stated, he wished he had never found himself in that situation; forced into it as he had been, he had no choice than to play by the rules of the game.

After his brutal war experiences, he personally wished that that heinous and barbaric conflict that brought untold suffering to millions worldwide would be the last war to be fought on earth – wishful thinking, as he would soon realise.

* * *

Life in the army was not only regimented; soldiers were expected to display a high standard of discipline.

Kakra was generally likeable, as he was when growing up in his little village.

Readers will recall that he did not receive any formal education. Some of his playmates, including Kofi Ofori, who as readers may also recollect, taught him to read and write, returned from school to report about being subjected to corporal punishment – caning – at school. Well, if only for that reason, he counted himself blessed.

Not that he could entirely reckon with being spared the whip at home – far from it! Indeed, on not a few occasions Duku resorted to the cane in an attempt to contain the misdemeanours of his mischievous little boys.

Kakra and Panin on their part sought to take advantage of their stunning resemblance to each other to escape punishment. One way they went about it was for both of them to simultaneously own up to an offence that had evidently been committed by just one individual!

With Panin no longer around to team up with him to play tricks on whoever wanted to subject him to discipline, for whatever reasons, Kakra had no choice but to abide by the military rules, or face the consequences.

The soldier could be sanctioned individually on the following grounds: disobedience of command, wearing dirty clothes, drunken behaviour, theft, murder, etc. Soldiers could also be punished as a group on the grounds of collective insubordination or mutiny.

Minor offences or cases were dealt with by a commissioned or non-commissioned officer as the case might be. Serious cases, on the other hand, were brought before a military court-martial.

Punishment usually involved caning and was administered instantly, usually by a non-commissioned officer. As Kakra would found out, punishment was meted out not only in peacetime but also in the heat of war.

Apart from a few reprimands he received for turning up a few minutes late for training, Kakra stayed, generally, out of trouble throughout his time in the army.

Chapter 9
The race of the martials

—mm—

IT WAS NOTED earlier that the majority of the new conscripts who joined Kakra to swear the oath of allegiance were Muslims. As Kakra soon found out, almost all those in that group were members of the Hausa ethnic group – spread out in the Sahel Zone of West Africa. In the Gold Coast, they were found predominantly in the Northern territory.

What had led to the over-representation of the Hausas in the army, Kakra wondered? Had a Hausa traditional leader been overambitious in his desire to fulfil his quota, in return for even more favours from the colonial masters, perhaps?

In the course of time Kakra gained further insight into the matter. He came to understand that it wasn't accidental that the Hausas were over-represented in the army. It was indeed part of the recruiting strategy of the British.

As Kakra gathered in the course of his service, the British, after observing members of the various ethnic groups of their various colonies, had come to the realisation that some members of specific ethnic groups were more suited to serve as soldiers than others.

The fact that they regarded the members of the identified ethnic groups to be more suitable for military service was not necessarily based on physique or the appearance of strength. Rather, it was based on the attitude of the various ethnic groups to various situations in life.

The British basically classified members of the various ethnic groups in their colonies into two groups.

The first group consisted of those whose members adopted an easy-going, laissez-faire attitude to life – members of that group were avoided in the recruitment drive.

The second group was made up of ethnic groups whose members were found to possess characteristics that could be described as steady and reliable. Members of this category were found to be amenable to discipline, obedient to command, capable of enduring extreme and challenging conditions without much complaining, capable of marching great distances with few provisions as well as sturdy in battle, etc. To describe this group, the British coined the term 'martial race'. As might be expected, the individuals from such ethnic groups were given preference when it came to military recruitment.

In West Africa, the colonial masters identified members of the Hausa ethnic group as possessing the cherished qualities of the martial races!

As Kakra learnt in the course of his time in the army, up until the increased demand for troops brought about by the events of the Second World War forced the British to look beyond the Hausa ethnic group for conscripts from population groups such as the Akans, Gas and Ewes, the Hausa formed the core ethnic group of the Royal West African Frontier Force (RWAFF).

As Kakra interacted with the British soldiers on the battlefield in the course of the war, he wondered where to place them on his own imaginary grading scale depicting the qualities of the martial race, ranging from zero (the least preferred) to 10 (the most preferred) – Grade 3, perhaps?

Chapter 10
The homesick dreamer

IN THE FIRST FEW WEEKS of his conscription, Kakra felt terribly homesick. Though Nyamekye turned out to be a great companion in need, he could not fill the emotional void that the absence of Panin had created in Kakra.

Besides Panin, the next family member he missed most was their two years' younger sister Tawiah. On several occasions he dreamt about home, dreams that involved interactions with various members of both his nuclear and extended family members.

In one such dream, he was sitting before his parents, Asoh and Duku.

Duku began to address him: "We have closely observed your ways since the tragic events surrounding your capture. More than six months after your capture you do not seem to be able to overcome your ordeal – you are so sad, you're not eating properly. Just take a look in the mirror. You are just a bag of bones, a dead man walking in the real sense of the word.

"As might be expected, we are deeply concerned about your health, Kakra. Our fear is that if things continue this way, you may one day collapse and die."

"Don't worry, Papa, all will be fine!" he replied.

"All cannot be fine so long as you are not eating properly, Kakra!" Asoh cut in.

"I *am* eating!"

"Eating – what?"

"The food you cook!"

"What have you eaten today?"

"I ate part of the meal of *Ampesi,* the boiled yams and the sauce you prepared for dinner."

"How many pieces of yam did you eat?"

"Half a piece."

"Half a piece! That is nothing for even a child, altogether insufficient for someone your age!"

"It's not my fault, Mama."

"Whose fault then?"

"Just as I swallow the food down my throat, the image of Panin flashes through my mind. I imagine I can hear him whispering in a sad, low voice in my ears: 'You are eating, Kakra, while your brother Panin is starving to death!'"

Hearing this, tears dropped from Asoh's eyes. "Duku!" she began, wiping the tears from her eyes with the *ntamah* wrapped around her waist. "Let's take your son to a traditional healer; he seems to be losing his mind!"

"Who is losing his mind?" Kakra asked.

"Yourself!"

"No, I am fine, Mama, I am fine!"

"Well, Kakra, both of us have pondered over your situation for a while", Duku said, re-joining the conversation. "We have come to the conclusion that you need a companion, a close companion like Panin to help you cope with the boredom of military life."

"A companion? What do you mean by a companion? I have a lot of mates in the army."

"No, you need a beautiful wife to keep you comfortable."

At that moment Asoh opened a door, and in came an attractive, cheerful-looking young woman about his age. She gave him a broad smile on seeing him, in the process displaying her brilliantly white teeth.

"This is an Asante princess, a royal girl, the daughter of Omanhene of Kyerekwie traditional area. She is a present for you!"

Kakra's heart leapt on seeing her.

He immediately got up. With his arms outstretched, he moved towards her with the intention of embracing and kissing her. Just then his eyes opened!

53

"Damn it!" he cried out in fury.

His loud cry aroused a good number of his mates from their sleep!

"What is that matter with you?" Kofi Awartey inquired.

"Nothing!"

"Sure?"

"Yes."

"Why do you keep on screaming and shouting in your sleep if indeed everything is okay!?" Nii Odametey burst out.

"Maybe we should take him to the military doctor", Yaw Bonsu suggested.

"Yes indeed", Nii Odametey concurred. "Before our friend goes really crazy and points his gun at us."

The others burst into laughter.

"Hey guys, you are disturbing my sleep", Musah, one of the recruits, who even prior to the incident had been tossing and turning on his mat as he struggled to sleep, protested.

Before long silence returned to the hall.

On another occasion Kakra dreamt that his sister Tawiah was taking part in the puberty rite ceremony, which consists of a set of rituals that an Akan girl experiencing her menstrual period for the first time had to undergo to be formally initiated into womanhood.

Akan society expects every girl to undergo the *Bragoro* ritual before being given in marriage. The climax of the event is preceded by several days of preparation. During the time of preparation, the participants withdraw from society for a while to be mentored by the queen mother of the community or a few selected elderly women chosen by the initiates to represent them.

During the training period, which may last between two and three weeks, the partakers are mentored on matters pertaining to womanhood, indeed on the distinguishing characteristics or qualities of a woman.

The elderly women, based on their own experience, attempt to impart to the young, would-be wives and mothers, their respective insights into matters relating to sexual relationship, pregnancy, child birth, child upbringing, wife–husband relationships, etc.

After periods of seclusion and training the group of young girls are finally presented to the society in a colourful ceremony – the *Bragoro* ceremony proper.

Amid drumming and dancing, the young women, scantily yet colourfully dressed, dance rhythmically to the sound of drums and traditional music.

Tawiah, who though a reluctant partaker – indeed she would have avoided it if she had her own way – nevertheless discharged her societal duty with impressive bravado. As Duku and Asoh and the rest of her siblings – Panin, Nyankomagoh, Baffour Anane and Nana Yaw – looked on, she danced to the various tunes of traditional music.

After several hours going through one ritual after the other, the day was finally over for Tawiah. She was proud that at long last she would no longer be regarded as a girl, but could instead be counted among the women of the community.

That very night of the initiation ceremony, Duku and Asoh gathered all leading members of the family together and presented Tawiah to Panin in marriage!

Kakra was furious! How could his parents offer his and Panin's sister to Panin, her brother, in marriage! As he protested vehemently, the wake-up trumpet for the recruits sounded.

Throughout the day, Kakra pondered over the dream, wondering what it could mean!

After undergoing training in the grasslands along the Atlantic coast, the recruits were told to prepare for jungle warfare in an unknown location.

At around 4 a.m. the next day, their wake-up trumpet was sounded. They had hardly 15 minutes to get ready for the journey. Soon the military convoy of a dozen vehicles was set in motion.

After driving for about an hour they were asked to disembark on the edges of a thick forest. They were then marched into the middle of the forest. Moments later they got to work, setting up a camp within the thick jungle.

The training in jungle warfare involved not only how to fight the enemy in the jungle but also how to survive in the dense and tangled vegetation when cut off from the rest of the troops.

Among the survival tips, they were taught how to identify edible plants and fruits, how to track and trap animals, collect water and build a fire in the challenging terrain.

After spending six weeks in the jungle, Commander Cobra assembled his men around him one morning and began:

"After undergoing six weeks' gruelling exercises in the dense and thick vegetation, I am confident the experience you have gained has been invaluable and will enable you to survive and fight in whatever jungle terrain, however challenging, you will be exposed to."

He paused for a while and looked around. There was deep silence. Then he continued:

"I really wish I could dismiss you back to camp to enable you to enjoy a period of rest – but unfortunately I have received instructions from command headquarters ordering me to move you immediately to a suitable location to offer you training in a terrain displaying plateaus, plains and highlands."

"This is in response to worrying intelligence that points to signs of an imminent invasion of British Somaliland by the Fascist Mussolini. The Empire may need additional troops from West Africa to ward off the invasion. Subsequently I have been instructed to give you the necessary training to help you become accustomed to that type of environment."

Without further ado, that very night they were driven to a location that had a suitable terrain to continue the military training.

PART 2
EAST AFRICAN CAMPAIGN

Chapter 11
Mobilising against Fascist aggression

~mm~

I T WAS SEPTEMBER 14, 1940.
Nine months had passed since his conscription into the RWAFF
against his will. Though still a reluctant soldier, he had gradually come
to terms with his situation. Some of his mates, especially those who
hailed from the immediate surroundings, had applied for and were
granted leave. As he later found out, this applied only to those who had
signed up voluntarily; indeed, he had in the meantime found out from
interacting with his fellow soldiers that not everyone was there against
his will. In fact, some had travelled considerable distances to apply to
join the army. That anyone would surrender himself of his own accord
– and based on their own accounts, willingly and in an enthusiastic
manner – to undergo such an intense and arduous military programme
of training and be subjected to the regimented lifestyle of a soldier, was
something Kakra found hard to comprehend.

When he asked them for their motivation, he received diverse
answers, such as:

1. The khaki uniform of soldiers served as an attraction to women;
2. It offered employment opportunities; or
3. Young men enlisted simply out of youthful exuberance.

Thus, though not laid bare as official policy, those who were there
of their own accord were granted the privilege of periods of short home

leave; on the other hand requests for home leave from those who were there against their will were rejected – without explanation.

Kakra had thought the day would be like any other day; but that did not prove to be the case. After the early morning training, the young recruits were asked to gather in a hall to await an important announcement from a visiting high-ranking military officer.

After he had been introduced by Commander Cobra, Lt General Smith, alias Lt Gen Leopard, the visiting officer, began to address them.

"Men, are you prepared for action?"

"Yeah, yeah!" the voices of several hundred young recruits yelled back.

"Okay, then get ready. Word has reached us from military headquarters in Freetown, Sierra Leone, to move camp! We are heading for East Africa, in the service of the Empire!"

He paused a moment to gauge the reaction of the troops. There was eerie silence in the large hall.

He continued:

"It is important that I give you some background information about the campaign we are about to become involved in. To help you get a better picture of what it entails, I have brought along a map of East Africa."

At that stage, he beckoned to two men sitting in the front row to come forward.

They did as requested.

Next, he unfolded a large map of East Africa which he held in his hands and asked the two to help him hang it on a large display board.

The two quickly got the job done.

"Thank you very much; get back to your seats", he instructed them.

When everyone was seated and silence had returned to the hall, Lt Gen Smith began to address them. Making use of a long thin pointer in his right hand, he began to explain to his men the conflict zones of East Africa and the possible areas they could be called upon to serve.

"It is quite a complicated matter", he began. "I do not want to go into details in order not to confuse you. What is important as far as you are concerned is the following:

"In December 1935 Benito Mussolini, the Fascist leader of Italy, invaded Abyssinia. As expected, the Abyssinians initially resisted the invasion. In the end, however, they proved to be no match for the well-equipped forces of the aggressor. On May 5, 1936, the invading forces finally entered Addis Ababa, the Abyssinian capital; with that move, the Italian conquest of Abyssinia was sealed. Haile Selassie, the Abyssinian Emperor, was forced into exile on the same day.

"Prior to the invasion and subsequent conquest of Abyssinia, Italy had colonised Italian Somaliland and Eritrea. How they came to colonise the two territories I have just referred to is not relevant to our present discussion.

"With the conquest of Abyssinia, which as you can see from the map, borders on Italian Somaliland and Eritrea, a large swathe of the territory of East African came under Italian control. The area subsequently became known as Italian East Africa.

"Nestled between Italian East Africa, French Somaliland and the sea, is British Somaliland.

So – if only the Fascist Mussolini could be satisfied with the booty he had acquired through aggression! But no! In line with the expansionist ideas of both himself and Adolf Hitler, the treacherous Mussolini has chosen to invade British Somaliland.

"Partly as a result of the long frontier between British Somaliland and Italian East Africa (Italian Somaliland, Italian Eritrea and Abyssinia), and also due to the fact of the impending conflict being very unexpected, it was thought prudent to withdraw Empire forces in the territory across the Gulf of Aden to the neighbouring Empire colony of Aden instead of putting them in harm's way.

EAST AFRICAN CAMPAIGN

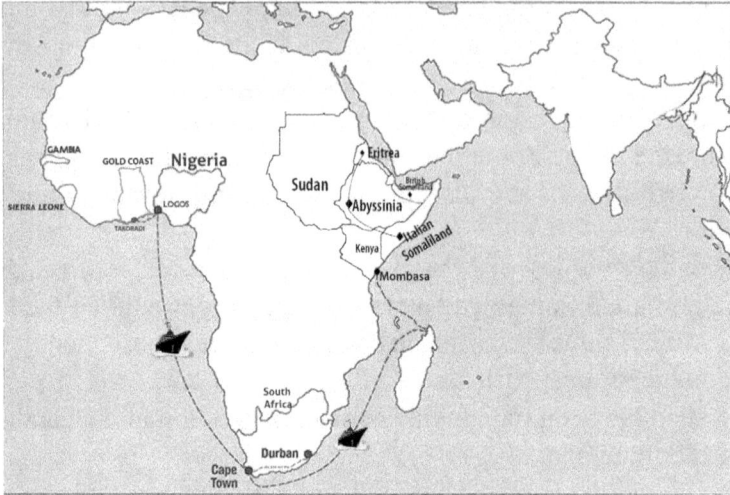

Gold Coast NOW Ghana
Abyssinia NOW Ethiopia

"Now, looking at the map, you will realise that Italian East Africa is bordered to the south by Kenya and the west by Sudan. Kenya is Empire territory, a member of the British Commonwealth. Sudan on its part is jointly controlled by Britain and Egypt.

"As everyone is aware, Mussolini, in line with his expansionist ideas, will not be satisfied with his present gains. The Empire needs to act swiftly not only to dislodge his forces from British Somaliland, but also to prevent them from further incursions into additional Empire territory in East Africa, in particular Kenya.

"As I speak, Empire forces are engaged in fierce battles with Hitler on mainland Europe. Partly as a result of this, and also considering the climatic and geographical conditions of East Africa, it has been decided to employ Empire forces in Africa to help expel Mussolini from the African continent.

"You must bear in mind the ulterior motive of Fascist Mussolini and Hitler in Africa – the total enslavement of the whole continent.

"Defeat of Mussolini and Hitler is victory not only for Europe but for Africa as a whole. So we are going to fight to liberate Africa!"

He paused and surveyed the sea of faces before him. All eyes were fixed on him. "My men", he said into the pregnant silence. "Are we all prepared – if need be – to make the ultimate sacrifice to prevent that from happening, is that right?"

There was no response.

"Let me put the question to you once again. I want you to shout three yeahs as a sign of approval.

"My men, are we all prepared – if need be – to make the ultimate sacrifice to prevent that from happening, is that right?"

"Yeah, yeah, yeah!!" they all screamed back.

"Okay, then get ready for action. By the latest in three days we will be moving camp, heading for faraway East Africa!"

Soon the meeting came to an end.

That night as the recruits began packing their items, a lively discussion ensued among them.

"White man, my brothers – trouble, trouble makers!" Abubakari, one of the recruits began in broken English.

"Real trouble makers." Kakra, whose knowledge of the English language was steadily improving thanks to the twice-weekly English language classes recruits had to attend, agreed. "They begin a fight in Europe; they bring the fight to Africa; now by force they want Africans to join in the fight!"

"My brother, you can say that again!" Tanko, a stoutly built Hausa recruit, joined in the discussion.

"Why they no fight their own fight, but send us to go and die; for what?" Nando, a conscript from Tamale, the main city of the northern territory, a member of the Dagomba ethnic group, wondered.

"As for me, if I get chance I will *commot* and go home", Abubakari revealed.

"*Commot*, what do you mean by *commot*?" Nando inquired.

"No understand *commot*? Means... run, run!"

"*Commot!!* Abubakari's own English for run away?" Kakra queried.

"Yeah, yeah!"

"Me too, if I get chance, I will *commot*!!" Kakra declared.

Escaping! It was mere wishful thinking, and everyone present knew that. As already mentioned, the camp was surrounded by a barbed wire fence. Not only that, it was guarded round the clock by specially selected soldiers with proven loyalty to King and Empire. Still, a few recruits had been caught attempting with primitive instruments to cut through the barbed wire.

The punishment for whoever attempted to escape was detention for a specific period of time, during which time the recruit lost almost every privilege.

Just as their commander had announced, three days later they set out on their journey to East Africa.

Their journey began in a military convoy of several vehicles that drove them from their training grounds in a camp near Accra, the Gold Coast capital, to Takoradi, a harbour town situated about 200 kilometres to the west of Accra.

Initially the plan was for them to board troopships directly on their arrival from Accra.

It was when they were on their way that word reached their superiors to the effect that the arrival of their troopships would be delayed for a few days. Instead of heading straight to the seaport, the convoy was subsequently diverted to the Takoradi military barracks. There the troops set up camp, pending the arrival of their ship.

Chapter 12
A West African coastal town's invaluable yet hardly recognised Second World War contribution

—*mm*—

T HE DELAY provided the troops heading for East Africa the opportunity, not only to familiarise themselves with the barracks but also to interact with the soldiers at the base.

As they neared the barracks, Kakra's attention was drawn to the frenetic activities going on, in the camp and in the adjoining military airfield.

Also conspicuous was the presence not only of several white military personnel but several Royal Air Force aircraft parked on the airfield. As might be expected, the curiosity of the new arrivals, Kakra included, was aroused by the unusual scene.

In the course of their stay, Kakra and his mates, through conversation with the indigenous soldiers at the base, got to know the reason for the presence of the considerably large number of foreign troops there.

As a result of hostilities between Allied Forces, made up of the Empire, the US (which had in the meantime joined in the conflict) and other European countries on the one side and the forces of the Axis (Germany, Italy and Japan) on the other, in and around the Mediterranean, it was considered unsafe for Allied ships to sail through the Mediterranean Sea to deliver supplies to Allied forces in the Middle East.

The alternative sea route was via Africa's Cape of Good Hope and the Red Sea. Not only were there no ships available to carry the planes along the long route, the voyage itself would have taken three to four months – a long period of time that would have given the enemy a huge advantage over Allied troops!

In their desperate search for an alternative route to deliver much needed supplies to their forces in the shortest possible time, the Allied military leadership developed the so-called West African Reinforcement Route, with both the sea and airports of the Gold Coast town of Takoradi playing a pivotal role in the concept.

From Britain, fighter aircraft were transported in crated form along the Atlantic ocean to the seaport of Takoradi. On their arrival, the aeroplanes were assembled and flown northwards, over a 6000-kilometre air route that went over the Sahara desert to the Egyptian town of Abu Suweir. Located about 116 kilometres to the north-east of Cairo and strategically positioned for the defence of the Suez Canal waterway, the Abu Suweir Air Base served as a military airfield for both the Royal Air Force (RAF) and the United States Air Force during their North Africa Campaign against Axis forces.

The strategic location of Takoradi served the US Army war effort as well.

US aircraft being transported on ships from the US via ports along the eastern Brazilian coastline to supply war zones in Sudan, Egypt and the Mediterranean used the seaport of Takoradi as a transit base.

In this way, not only did the ships avoid the need to embark on the long North Atlantic crossing to reach their destination, but also the possible dangers posed by the German Air Force (*Die Luftwaffe*) over the Mediterranean.

Beside the seaport, the US army utilised the Takoradi airport as a major refuelling stop for flights between their air bases in Monrovia, Liberia and Lagos, Nigeria. (From Lagos the planes flew further north to supply Allied forces in Sudan, Egypt and the Middle East.)

Not only did the British and the US military utilise the strategic location of Takoradi for their respective Second World War efforts – the South African military did so as well. Takoradi served as a base for the 26 Squadron of the South African Air Force (SAAF). From there Vickers Wellington bombers took off on their anti-submarine and convoy protection patrol flights over the Atlantic.

In the course of their short stay, Kakra also had the opportunity to speak to some of the few women who happened to be in the area – nurses, as he found out. They bore witness to another enemy which was making life difficult for the soldiers, especially the foreigners – diseases such as malaria, yellow fever, blackwater fever, septicaemia and pneumonia. The nurses went on to state that a good many of the foreign soldiers had already succumbed to some of the diseases mentioned.

Chapter 13
Kakra's premier at sea experience

~~~

Eleven days after the day of their arrival, the order came for them to get ready for the departure on the next day.

It was a bright morning with a clear blue sky when they boarded the troopships taking them to their unknown destination. Relatives of some of the recruits had turned up at the port to bid their loved ones farewell.

If travelling on an ordinary vehicle was an exciting first-time experience for Kakra, he had to get ready for a more thrilling encounter – namely his maiden voyage on a ship!

It was a little past 10:30 in the morning when the ship weighed anchor and steamed graciously along the vast ocean mass of the Atlantic. A cool refreshing breeze blew in the face of the novice as the landmass gradually receded from view.

At that moment, the thought of Panin came to mind. How were he and the family getting on with life without him? Would he ever see them again? Or would this voyage be the last time he would ever see the Gold Coast?

His body system would not allow him the peace to contemplate his situation further, for just at that juncture he began all of a sudden to feel dizzy. With the slow lurching of the ship and the rise and fall of the horizon he also felt like vomiting.

Just before they set off, each of them had been given a pill to swallow. "It is to prevent sea sickness", the military nurse who distributed the medication had told them.

Though he had dutifully followed the instructions and swallowed the pill, it appeared ineffectual! As he would soon find out, it was not only himself who was battling with the condition, for quite a good number of the conscripts were reporting similar symptoms.

Much as he tried to suppress the mounting urge to vomit, he soon realised he could not do so for long and he dashed for the lavatory! He got there just in time to prevent having to vomit on others.

After a while he recovered sufficiently to return to the deck to interact with other mates gathered in groups there. Just as in his case, the uncertainty of what awaited them occupied the minds of each of them.

The journey up the coast lasted several days. Everything was new: the waves, which came smashing against the exterior of the ship and tossed it about like a cork, the refreshing cool breeze, the clean smell of salt in the air.

Conditions on the ship were basic, nothing luxurious – just what was necessary to sustain them during the journey.

As they journeyed along the vast watery mass, over the great ocean that appeared endless, the ship with its human cargo crammed onto the deck and compartments beneath the deck appeared to Kakra to be no more than a tiny dot on the huge expanse of water.

Initially everyone slept in the holds below deck; after a few days on the journey, the captain permitted those who desired to do so to sleep on the deck.

Kakra took advantage of the latter opportunity and spent the nights sleeping with several others in the open; on nights devoid of clouds he was mesmerised by the clear star-studded night sky.

After sailing for several days, the vessel made a short stop at Durban before sailing on to their final destination, the port of Mombasa in Kenya.

From Mombasa, they travelled further inland by train. Their final destination was a military base a few kilometres away from Kenya's frontier with Italian East Africa.

Chapter 14
Fascist Italy biting off more than it can chew

⁓⁓⁓

I N JANUARY 1941, British forces launched a counter offensive against Italian forces in Italian East Africa. From Sudan in the north, British forces advanced into Eritrea. Battling through mountainous territory, they captured the heavily garrisoned town Agordat from the Italians. At the same time that Italian East Africa was being pounded by British forces from the north, an assault was also launched from the south from Kenya by West African and South Africa troops.

The troops of the Royal West African Frontier Force had been divided into the 1st (African) and 2nd (African) Divisions and placed under the overall command of the British military officer, Lieutenant General Cunningham.

Kakra was assigned to the 1st Division; Nyamekye on his part was placed in the 2nd Division.

Lieutenant General Cunningham personally took control of one of the groups, the group to which Kakra belonged. Whereas his group headed east, towards Italian Somaliland, the remaining group to which Nyamekye belonged marched northwards into Abyssinia.

On February 10, Lieutenant General Cunningham's men, attacking from Kenya, overran Italian positions at Jilib, a Somaliland township not very far from the Kenyan frontier. From Jilib, the unit pursued the retreating Italians further north along the Jilib to Mogadishu road. On February 26, Mogadishu, the capital, fell to them.

On March 5, the Italian army lost control of the whole of Italian Somaliland.

At that stage, Lieutenant General Cunningham further divided his troops into two; he led one group further northwards; the other, to which Kakra was a part, advanced north-west into Abyssinia.

On one occasion, the makeshift base of Kakra's unit came under intense bombardment from the Italian Air force, which resulted in some casualties. They might have been completely annihilated by the enemy, had it not been for the forewarning they received by way of a radio message from their air surveillance division minutes prior to the arrival of the enemy planes.

For a small fraction of his mates, the warning did not come early enough. Indeed, whereas the great majority of the unit managed to escape into the protective shelter of a makeshift bunker they had constructed days before, a small proportion of them could not make it in time and were either injured or killed.

Eventually Kakra's group caught up with the group that had earlier on been sent north from Kenya. They engaged in joint manoeuvres, in preparation for their assault on Addis Ababa.

Kakra's group had reckoned with fierce resistance from the Italian forces. Contrary to their expectations, however, on April 6, 1941, the group captured the Abyssinian capital Addis Ababa virtually unopposed, the Italian garrison originally based in the city having withdrawn to battlefields in the north of the country.

This would become a general feature of the campaign – overall the Italians offered less resistance than the British troops had envisaged.

Defending the whole of their self-declared Italian East Africa clearly put the Italian forces under a great strain. As it turned out, Italy seemed to have bitten off more than it could chew. The insurgents or partisans resisting their presence in Abyssinia were putting up a real fight. Keen on consolidating their positions in Abyssinia, they committed a considerable amount of manpower and material to that cause. In the end, they were routed earlier than Kakra and his mates had anticipated.

Though much of the fighting to regain control of Addis Ababa from the Italian occupants was done by the West African troops spearheaded by troops from Nigeria, the victory march into the city painted a different picture.

To the utter dismay of the West African troops, their white commanders prevented them from marching ahead of the victory parade into the city. It was instead white South African soldiers who were given the privilege to march in front, leaving the gallant West African soldiers to march far behind, creating the impression that their white counterparts from the southern tip of the continent had played a leading role in the conflict.

"That is really annoying!" Mutara, a Nigerian soldier who in the meantime had become a good pal of Kakra, protested bitterly.

"One person suffers for another person to enjoy the rewards, eh?" His anger was written on his face.

"That indeed is what it all boils down to. They send us ahead to do the dirty job, and now they are marching ahead as heroes!"

"Oga, I have observed one thing. Why are the South Africans not allowing any black men in their fighting division?"

"My friend, why you ask me? Go ask them yourself!"

"So dey think black man no be able to fight war?"

"Probably; otherwise they wouldn't exclude them from their fighting force."

"But they are witnesses to the gallantry of the African soldiers, aren't they?"

"Well, they don't recognise it! Otherwise they wouldn't have prevented the Nigerians from leading the triumphal march into Addis Ababa."

Following the capture of Addis Ababa, Haile Sellaise made a triumphal return to the capital on May 5, 1941 – exactly five years to the day Italian forces moved into the city and forced him into exile.

Several soldiers of the RWAAF, including Kakra, were selected to form a guard of honour to welcome him back home.

The battle to regain control of Addis Ababa had been decided in favour of the Allied forces; but the war was not over yet, for Italian forces still controlled large swathes of northern Abyssinian.

The Allied forces did not relent in their effort and pursued them still, leading to the fall of their bases in the northern Abyssinian towns of Amba Alagi (in May) and Jimma (in July).

The retreating forces converged on the mountain town Gondar, the capital of Amhara.

In what can aptly be described as the climax of the campaign, the attacking Allied forces and the recalcitrant Italians guarding it, met in a fierce battle on November 27, 1941, which saw the surrender of the Italian forces, and in effect the end of their presence in Italian East Africa.

Chapter 15
West African troops and colour discrimination

—mm—

As mentioned in the previous chapter, a good deal of the fight to liberate Abyssinia from Italian control was carried out by West African troops, in particular Nigerian troops. In the end they proved the sceptics, indeed those who harboured reservations about their soldiering capabilities, wrong.

As Kakra's English commander revealed to his men, men who by virtue of their extraordinary bravery had endeared themselves to his heart, at the outset the General Officer Commanding (GOC) of the British East African Force, Lieutenant General Cunningham, had actually favoured the deployment of white South African troops on the frontline instead of Africans on the grounds that the South Africans were supposedly better equipped and mechanised vis-à-vis the Africans. As it turned out, it was an excuse, indeed a pretext, to conceal the real motive behind the directive – prejudice against the African soldiers.

Among other things, the military hierarchy held the prejudicial view that the African would not be reliable on the war-front, indeed that he was incapable of standing up to the challenging battlefield situation outside of his native bush, and was in fact not able to cope with the challenges posed by a demanding modern battlefield scenario, situations that would require the soldier simultaneously to be in a position to deal with multiple dangers – even manifold dangers in the form of air bombardment, artillery shelling, machine gunfire, etc.

Still other supposed shortcomings that were cited as factors spoke of the perceived unsuitability of Africans to engage in action on frontline duty – of their supposed inability to endure water shortages and to brave adverse conditions posed by the freezing temperatures of high altitude.

In the end, the brave Africans proved the cynics wrong, managing well even when their water supplies dwindled, excelling in unfamiliar terrains such as that prevailing in the Marda Pass in Abyssinia, a route through mountain ranges with elevations of well over 1800 metres above sea level.

And how did the white South African, the preference of the military authorities, perform?

It was no secret that the two South African brigades that took part in the battle to take control of Addis Ababa did not perform as well as anticipated. On the other hand, even the sceptics had to acknowledge the brilliant display of military prowess manifested by the fearless soldiers from Nigeria.

Chapter 16
The tragic end of a hero

~~~

Though fighting in two different divisions, Kakra, initially, was in quite regular contact with Nyamekye. This was maintained until shortly after the Battle of Gondar. To break the resistance of a recalcitrant Italian force unwilling to surrender, even in the face of obvious defeat, Nyamekye's unit was ordered to proceed to an area held by the defiant unit.

That was the last time Kakra was to see him. As he later learnt from Ndidi, a Nigerian mate of his, their unit was ambushed by a group of Italian soldiers who had taken up a position in a cave in a mountainous terrain. According to Ndidi's account, Nyamekye was killed instantly by a grenade that exploded just beside him. Sadly, the surviving members of the unit were unable to retrieve the bodies of their fallen heroes.

Kakra was heartbroken at the news of the passing away of his very dear friend. Did he ever come to terms with it? Hardly – if his emotional reactions to the memory of that incident is anything to go by.

Indeed, throughout his life, every time he recounted his war experiences, he could hardly hold back his tears when he came to this point in the narration.

Chapter 17
Brass band and patriotic music for the heroic returnees

~~~

HAVING SUCCESSFULLY liberated Italian East Africa and
British Somaliland from Italian control, it was time for the gallant
and victorious African soldiers to head back home. In early 1942 the
West Africa brigades embarked on their homeward journey. The evening
prior to the day of departure, a farewell parade was held.

Lieutenant General Cunningham, their GOC, was there in person to
bid them farewell and address them as follows:

"Men, on behalf of King and Empire, I want to thank you very
much for your courage and bravery. With your help East Africa has been
liberated from Fascist aggression! Now it is time to go back home, to
loved ones, indeed to your various communities. It is my sincere hope
you will not be called upon to embark on a similar mission again.

"Fare thee well, fearless soldiers. The Empire is really proud of you!"

So finally, in the early hours of a February morning in 1942, Kakra's
unit set sail back to West Africa.

They took the same route as on the outbound trip, but this time in
reverse order.

They were transported in a convoy of military trucks, first to
Mombasa where they boarded their troopship.

After stops in Durban and Lagos, the ship finally docked at the port
of Takoradi shortly before Easter Day 1942.

Kakra was elated to step back on to the shores of the Gold Coast. The welcoming committee of the military had organised a brass band to play patriotic music to welcome the gallant troops back home. Some relatives and friends, especially those who resided in the urban areas, had got word of their arrival and had turned up at the Takoradi harbour to welcome their loved ones back home.

Needless to say, there was no one there to greet Kakra. His family and friends had certainly no idea about his arrival back in the Gold Coast. Indeed, since the events of that fateful day in December, a little over two years previously, when he and his friend had been kidnapped, he had never had the opportunity to communicate with his family or anyone else in his home country. The main stumbling block in this regard was the absence of a post office in his community. As mentioned previously, the next available post office was in the district capital, Kofikrom. Either an individual or individuals, or the town committee acting on behalf of the whole town, could have rented a letter box there – but at the time that had not yet happened. Without a letter box, it was not possible for Kakra to communicate with his family by way of letters, in the way that several of his mates had done. Indeed, on a regular basis post arrived from home for his companions and was distributed to the men concerned on the battlefield. As might be expected, such letters were awaited with eager expectation by their recipients.

At the time of Kakra's return from East Africa, Takoradi was still playing a vital role in the Allied War efforts. Both the seaports and airports were still being used in various ways by the British, the US and the South African forces to advance their respective Second World War operations.

As Kakra learnt as he interacted with some of the servicemen, from the time of Takoradi's conception as a base in August 1940 up to the time of his return from East Africa, thousands of British planes such as Blenheims, Hurricanes and Spitfires, had already been assembled there and flown further to North Africa.

On their part, the US army had used the port as a transit and refuelling station for thousands of their Baltimore, Dakota, and Hudson planes on flights from Monrovia to Lagos.

With his own eyes Kakra saw many RAF planes, one after the other, taxi along the runway before lifting up into the skies, to disappear after a short while behind the clouds, heading for the war zones of North Africa along hazardous routes that included flying over the perilous, sandstorm-prone air space of the Sahara Desert.

As he watched the airfield bustling with activity from the open windows of the large building of the demobilisation centre, the important role Takoradi had been playing in the war raging in several places on the globe became even clearer to him.

Would the town along the West African coast receive its due recognition after the war, he wondered?

The plan was to keep the newly arrived soldiers at a holding centre especially prepared for them to allow them a few days respite before moving them further to their various military quarters from where they would either be discharged from the army or allowed to proceed on holidays.

Kakra eagerly yearned for his imminent reunion with his loved ones, in particular his twin brother Panin. As he did so, could he ever imagine the twists and turns in his personal fortunes that awaited him?

Chapter 18
A battle-proven soldier's fight against deadly micro-organisms

―*mm*―

A
S HE WAS REJOICING at the prospect of dismissal from the army and his subsequent return to the village, Kakra began to feel unwell.

It started with a fever. As was common in that part of the world, the initial assumption was that he had caught malaria. Consequently, he was treated with anti-malaria tablets, but instead of improving his condition worsened. Not only did the fever persist, he lost appetite and weight. At night, he was drenched in his own sweat.

He went to see the doctor again and was given various tests. Then, in one of his coughing fits, he began all of a sudden to cough up blood! He was immediately sent to see the military doctor.

The doctor requested an X-ray and a few other tests. Soon his suspicion was confirmed – Kakra had contracted lung tuberculosis! He was immediately placed into single isolation.

As he lay isolated in his hospital room, he had to battle not only with TB and the side-effects of its treatment, but also with symptoms of post-traumatic stress disorder which manifested itself, among others, in nightmares, sleep disorder, irritability, and feelings of guilt for being alive whilst others, like his close friend Nyamekye, had perished.

Not only that; he also felt home-sick and yearned to see his family, in particular Panin.

Since his return, he had sought ways of getting a message to his relative – in vain.

A few of his friends and acquaintances travelled as far as Kumasi to visit their relatives. None of them was willing however to travel the distance into the "bush" to deliver a letter to his relatives. They were ready to write and post letters, but as already mentioned, there was no way of getting the letters to them through a postal service.

With his almost complete isolation from the rest of the world, the prospect of getting in touch to his family – at least in the short and medium term – was almost non-existent.

Almost seven months of treatment followed, three of which involved his total isolation from the outside world.

Gradually, the isolation was lifted, permitting him to gradually associate with the outside world.

Finally, a few days before Christmas of 1942, he was declared completely cured of his ailment.

PART 3
BURMA CAMPAIGN

Chapter 19
Outburst of joy that turned out to be premature

—*wm*—

J ust as Kakra was rejoicing at the prospect of being discharged from hospital and enjoying a reunion with his family, one of his senior officers called on him one day and said:

"Well, unfortunately the news I am the bearer of will not be palliative to you."

"What is the matter?"

"Well, as you are aware, unfortunately, the Second World War is not over yet. With your help and sacrifice, the empire has managed to thwart Italian aggression in East Africa. However, the Empire needs your sacrifice yet another time."

"Not a second time! Please, please, leave me to go and see my family."

"We need to teach the Japanese lessons in combat! Just like Italy sought to encroach on Empire territory in East Africa, so Japan is aiming to do the same in Asia. Yes, the aggressor has invaded Burma. And that is only the first step – it's aiming at an even larger empire booty – India! Now the main army of the Empire of Britain is bogged down in a war with Hitler, in Europe. The onus has therefore fallen on Empire soldiers elsewhere to go to the aid of our compatriots in Burma.

"We have to save the Empire from Japanese aggression. Our main goal of engagement is to dislodge Japanese forces from the jungle and mountain ranges of Burma and in so doing prevent them from making further advances into India. By virtue of our geographical location, we are even more suited for the task.

"It is going to be a tough call, indeed a gruelling campaign which will involve among other things jungle marches, ambushes, battles, etc. But one thing is certain – we are going to overcome the enemy in the long run!"

"But I have gone through this serious disease TB. I don't feel strong enough to return to the battlefield!"

"Indeed, six months ago, we were considering dismissing you after your discharge from hospital. With the invasion of Burma by the Japanese, however, things have changed. We need men of your calibre, yes men with battlefield experience of the East African campaign, to teach the arrogant Japanese lessons in field combat.

"We have sought the opinion of the doctors on the matter.

"After carefully studying your medical notes, including your latest X-ray, they are of the opinion that you have made a complete recovery from the disease. They are of the opinion that based on your lung function, nothing stands in the way of your ability to assume your full military duties, including combat activities on the battlefield.

"They are only recommending a gradual build-up of your physical endurance over the next several days. That is exactly what is going to happen; in exactly a week from now you will rejoin your colleagues in our preparations."

Three years earlier, when he was told of the East Africa campaign, he was scared to death – no longer! Not only had he overcome the Italians in East Africa, he had also overcome the dreaded tuberculosis. Fear was not part of his mind-set; what would happen, would happen – whatever the consequences.

Chapter 20
A British military general drawing inspiration from African mythology

~~~

F RENETIC PREPARATION soon got underway in the camp with the goal of creating a fighting force for the Burma campaign. From several locations in the country, troops, both fresh conscripts as well as veterans from the East Africa campaign, poured into a military camp not far from the capital Accra.

On a day not long after the troops began arriving in the camp, they were asked to gather at their assembly point to await an important announcement.

Just as in the case of the East African campaign two years previously, with the help of a large map of South East Asia, a senior officer explained the mission ahead of them.

"As you are surely aware, the Second World War was begun by Adolf Hitler", he began his address. "He has in the meantime found allies in the person of Benito Mussolini and the Japanese under Emperor Hirohito.

"About two years ago the Royal West African Frontier Force (RWAAF) was called upon to help defend East Africa against Italian aggression. Quite a good number of you men took part in that operation.

"A similar situation has cropped up, though this one is outside the African continent.

"Japan has marched into Burma, which is Empire territory. Our mission is to help the Empire dislodge the occupying Japanese forces.

"I have received orders to move camp as soon as possible. We are not heading for the war zone – not yet. Instead, we are heading first to

Nigeria – to join our Nigerian comrades and other servicemen from the two remaining West African Crown colonies of Sierra Leone and the Gambia in an intense training exercise ahead of our mission to South East Asia."

Two days after the announcement, the troops left their military base at the outskirts of Accra and headed for Takoradi to board a ship for Lagos. From Lagos they were driven in a military convoy of several trucks to their final destination – a military training camp on the outskirts of Ede, a town located about 220 kilometres to the north east of Lagos.

As their officer had earlier pointed out, it was a multinational force comprised of troops from the four West African colonies of the Empire – Nigeria, the Gold Coast, Sierra Leone and the Gambia.

It came to be known as the British 81st (West Africa) Division and comprised of around 28,000 troops. It came under the command of Major General Christopher Geoffrey Woolner, a senior British Army officer who had already seen service in the First World War and had already spent five years in West Africa.

General Woolner chose a black spider on a yellow background as the divisional badge. He was led in his decision by the Akan mythology surrounding *Kwaku Anase*, the cunning spider capable of outwitting its enemies – both the weak and the mighty with con artistry and extraordinary skilful scheming. He hoped his men would draw inspiration from the Master Schemer in their impending encounters with the formidable Japanese foe.

Chapter 21
West African troops' dreadful encounters in segregated South Africa

~~~

After undergoing several weeks of intense jungle and weapon training, the first batch of troops were transported in a flotilla of six troopships and four destroyers; they set sail in early July 1943 from Lagos en route for their final destination in Bombay. It was the first time an African division of the British Empire was on a mission outside the African continent.

After several days on what seemed to be an unbounded mass of water, the troops finally saw in the distance the sign of land – the port of Cape Town as it turned out to be.

Though some of his mates who made stops there after them enjoyed a more favourable encounter with the locals, the Africans in Kakra's group were not well received. While the white officers were kindly received, the white residents queuing for an opportunity to take them on sightseeing trips into the countryside, even inviting them to their homes for dinners and parties, the blacks were given the cold shoulder. Indeed, initially the South African authorities refused to grant them permission to disembark. It was only after lengthy negotiations that they relented in their stance. Even then, they placed a restriction on the number of soldiers they would permit to leave the port at a time.

Kakra would in the course of their stay gain first-hand experience of racial prejudice that would linger in his memory long, long after his return to the Gold Coast. On the second day of their arrival, a contingent of his division was permitted to go on a march along the fringes of the city. As they marched along, in the company of their British colleagues, a white lady of middle age walked up to the white commanding officer and said:

"Sir, you surely are not going to entrust these monkeys with arms, are you?"

"Of course we will", he replied, taken aback. "They are frontier troops, committed soldiers ready to lay down their lives for King and Empire!"

"Placing weapons in the hands of monkeys! Ridiculous – totally ridiculous!" she countered, spitting on the ground apparently in a gesture meant to impart more weight to her scorn.

A group of Sierra Leonean soldiers also had their own story to tell:

"As we walked along the street, we felt the call of nature, so visited the nearest public toilet we came across. What we were not aware of was that it was a 'whites only' toilet! Just as we were in the middle of discharging 'our business' an elderly white man arrived. He was clearly infuriated on seeing us.

"Silly black men, why are you here? You better disappear immediately or I'll call the police!"

After spending four days in Cape Town, the ships sailed on. They made a further stop in South Africa, this time in Durban.

In contrast to the Cape Town experience, the troops were cordially welcomed in Durban. Without much ado, anyone wanting to disembark was granted permission to do so.

Kakra went window shopping with several other soldiers. The modern shops were filled with luxury goods of a type that fascinated him, and for the first time he experienced a ride in an elevator!

On their return, a group of Nigerian soldiers had their own dramatic story to tell.

"Friends, we nearly got ourselves into a palaver!"

"What palaver?" one of his listeners inquired.

"Well, you know back home in Lagos, we bargain for everything, don't we? I thought that was the situation here, so I asked the salesgirl to 'come down a bit' with the price of a piece of cake I had picked. She was really taken aback by my request.

"'It is a fixed price', she told me firmly.

"'That is too much.'

"'Okay, then put it back', she said.

"'But I need it', I insisted.

"'You either pay the amount or put it back; otherwise I will call security!'

"Well, a soldier man is a soldier man; I did not want to be intimidated by the officer who confronted me angrily. Soon an argument developed, which drew other shoppers to the scene.

"'What is the matter?' an elderly woman who later revealed that she had worked in the Gold Coast as a Catholic missionary inquired. On learning about the cause of the argument, she offered to pay not only for myself but purchased a piece of the cake for each member of the group!"

As already mentioned, a good proportion of the troops had earlier on served in East Africa. Somehow news got round to some of the South African troops who had also been to East Africa, that some of their former colleagues who were on their way to Burma had made a stop-over there. Soon quite a good number of them came to the port for a reunion with their former compatriots.

Chapter 22
Free language lessons on the high seas

~~~

F inally, Kakra's ship left Durban on the final leg of its journey. Was it out of despair, was it out of frustration, or was it out of fear of the unknown? The reason remains a mystery.

The fact is that, not long after the troopship set sail, a soldier, who as it turned out was from the Gold Coast and who for a while had been standing alone staring into the distance, all of a sudden screamed at the top of his voice: "I cannot leave my homeland!" And with that he leapt into the sea. Those whose attention had been aroused by his shout impulsively rushed to the scene – and he was nowhere to be found! The ship continued its journey as if nothing had happened.

As the ship sailed on, Kakra's heart was almost heartbroken as he pondered what had just befallen his comrade in arms. His thoughts went to the close relatives of the lost soldier. Would they ever realise that their loved one was lost at sea, indeed that his mortal remains were at rest somewhere in the deep, on the very floor of the Indian Ocean?

The Journey of Kakra to Burma

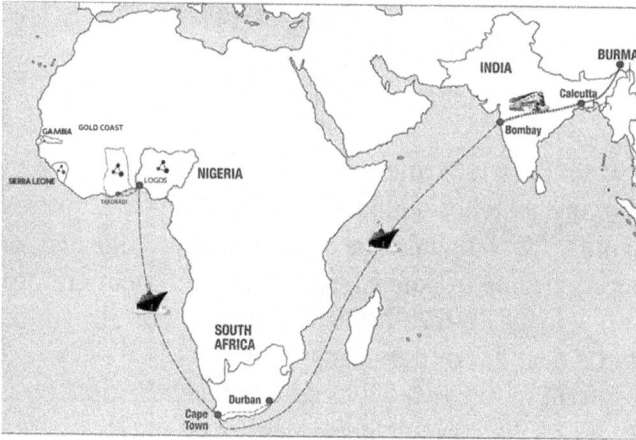

It was monotonous, really boring on the ship. To boost the spirits of the conscripts, a Catholic priest on board held regular morning prayer sessions for them. Though not forced to take part, quite a good deal of the Muslim soldiers also took part.

Though with certainty the author of the popular hymn 'Onward Christian Soldiers' did not have West Africa soldiers on a sea voyage to fight a war in the strange environment of Burma in mind at the time of writing the lines, yet many a soldier on board the ship heading for battle in an unknown land, regarded the hymn as a companion in need and recited or sang it day in and day out. In time, not only Kakra but a good many of them could recite at least the first verse, if not the whole of the hymn, by heart:

> Onward Christian soldiers!
> Marching as to war,
> With the cross of Jesus
> Going on before.
> Christ, the royal Master,
> Leads against the foe;
> Forward into battle,
> See, His banners go...

> Onward, Christian soldiers!
> Marching as to war,
> With the cross of Jesus,
> Going on before.

Other ways by which they sought to while away the time was by means of boxing matches and language lessons.

Concerning the language lessons, the few educated ones among them gathered groups of eager learners around them and tried to teach them not only to write the English alphabet, but also to learn simple English words needed for day-to-day use.

Kakra sought in his own way to drive away the time by learning the basic greetings in the various languages represented.

In the end, he became conversant in greetings in

Hausa...
mai kyau safe – Good morning
Barka da yamma – Good afternoon
Barka da yamma – Good evening
Allah ya ba mu alheri Mu kwana lafiya – Good night
Sai sannu Sai an jima Sai gobe – Goodbye

Yoruba...
Ẹ ku aarọ – Good morning
Ẹ ku ọsan – Good afternoon
Ẹ ku alẹ – Good evening
O da aarọ – Good night

and

Madinka(a.k.a Madingo)...

lisama	Good morning
Tilidiya	Good afternoon
Iwuvalara	Good evening

| Sutogediya | Good night |
| Fonyato | Good bye |

It was not a one-way street, however, for he also taught his mates who were interested to learn the basic greetings of his native **Twi** language:

Maakye – Good morning
Maaha – Good afternoon
Maadwo – Good evening
Dayie – Good night
Nante yie – Goodbye

In due course, not a few of the troops became polyglots, if only in regard to the basic greetings and expressions of the various West African languages represented.

Chapter 23
Bombay's odd reception for the strange human beings from a far distant land

—mm—

A fter sailing for a total of about six weeks, the flotilla of troopships finally docked at the port of Bombay on August 14, 1943.

Arrival of Kakra and part of the 81st
West African Division in Bombay.
(Source: Imperial War Museum K8860)

Kakra did not know what to expect in Bombay. As the reader is already aware, he did not get the opportunity to attend school. Though he had in the meantime acquired a basic knowledge in the English language, it was not sufficient to permit him, for example, to read about the leading Indian city in a book. As the reader is also aware, prior to his conscription in the army he had hardly travelled beyond the borders of his district.

Just as they got out of the harbour and in the escort of a special unit of the Indian army despatched to welcome them and take them to the train station to board the train to continue their journey, several children who had been playing on the streets on spotting them began to run after them.

The expressions on the faces of the children were of utter disbelief, on seeing their dark skin colour.

"Tails, tails, tails!" they kept on shouting.

"What tails?" Kakra and the others inquired in bewilderment.

"Monkey, monkey tail!"

"Which monkey?"

"Monkey, climbing trees!"

"What?"

"Well, I guess they think you are monkeys, endowed with tails", one of the Indians sent to escort them remarked.

"Tell them we are human beings; we don't have tails – only dark skin!"

The Indian escort translated this to the inquisitive children, by then a considerable number.

But no, they wouldn't be satisfied! Instead they kept on crying, "Monkeys' tails, monkeys' tails!"

In his exasperation one of the Africans attempted to give one of the children a knock on the head.

One of the Indian escorts reacted very quickly. Grasping the arm of the visitor he began:

"Please, please, be careful. It could lead to trouble; indeed we could be attacked by the mob!"

In response one of the Nigerian soldiers remarked:

"Never mind. We are soldiers. We are here to fight so it doesn't matter if we kick-start the war on the streets of Bombay!"

"Well, you are here to fight – but not to fight the Indians; rather, to help teach the Japanese lessons in good behaviour!"

"Then do teach your boys to behave!"

"Well, I will do my best, comrade!" the Indian escort reassured the Nigerian soldier whose feathers had been ruffled.

The scene just described would become a common pattern throughout their engagement in South East Asia.

From India to Burma, wherever they travelled, the curious crowd poured out into the streets to have a look at the "strange" beings on their streets.

FROM BOMBAY TO BURMA

BB BOMBAY*(Mumbai)*
NK NASIK
CA CALCUTTA
CG CHITTAGONG
CH CHIRINGA

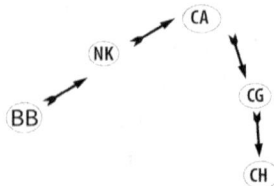

Kakra was struck by the number of beggars that lined the streets. Bombay was indeed a city of contrasts. Whereas some residents looked rich and well fed, the beggars lining the streets appeared emaciated. He could virtually count the bones of some of them.

The train took the African conscripts to Nasik, a town about 165 kilometres to the north east of Bombay. From there they were escorted a distance of about three miles away to Deolali transit camp on the outskirts of the Deolali township.

The camp was still under construction, but at least the bell-tents, each of which offered sleeping space for six soldiers, were already in place.

Kakra was housed with five other conscripts from the Gold Coast – three Hausas, one Frafra and one Ga.

Kakra's troopship was the first of many employed to transport the 81st Division from West Africa to Burma. In all it took about four months for the whole contingent to be assembled, the last ship docking in Bombay in November 1943.

As they waited for the arrival of the rest of their Division, those who had already arrived underwent further training in jungle warfare.

To while away the boredom brought about in part by the location's isolation and in part by its notoriety for its unpleasant environment, the troops constructed a football pitch, which enabled them to play football and also engage in other sporting activities commensurate with the facilities and means at their disposal.

Chapter 24
Kakra's 81st Division helps to bury the dead of a huge Indian metropolis

⁓m⁓

In the middle of November 1943, the order came for the 81st to move on to the next stage of their journey – a move towards the Burmese frontier. After spending about five days on the train, they arrived in Calcutta, about 1,800 kilometres to the north-east of Nasik.

If they were struck by the extent of begging that went on in Bombay, they would be even more astonished at the even larger number of beggars lining the streets of Calcutta.

Not only were they confronted with beggars wherever they went, they also saw a good number of people starving to death on the busy streets.

What also struck Kakra was the apparent disinterest of those who walked past the suffering individuals – had they become so used to the scene as to have grown immune to the human misery around them? It was a bitter reality that appeared very strange in the eyes of Kakra – that wealth and poverty could collide and co-exist in such close proximity to one another was beyond belief to him.

Kakra began to reflect on the situation. They had all been shipped at great cost over a vast distance to fight the Japanese in the jungles of Burma. Yet before their very eyes was a conflict that, at least based on what he was witnessing, had been left unaddressed.

Shouldn't the Empire launch another battlefront against another enemy bringing misery onto the streets of a major city within the Empire, namely, poverty?

Kakra became involved in the – undeclared, perhaps? – war he had just reflected upon in a way that he had not envisaged. To kill a bird with two stones, namely to occupy the idle hands of the West African soldiers and also to clear the streets of the starving and the dead, the West Africa troops were activated on two fronts:

One group was entrusted with the assisted removal and the transportation of the starving to camps to be fed and revived; a second group was charged with the collection of the bodies of those who had succumbed to the 'plague' of starvation for further transport into mass lime pits.

Babatunde, a Yoruba from Abeokuta in Nigeria known for his frank and outright talking, was quick to react to the situation.

"Friends, we did not travel all the way from West Africa to bury the Indian dead, did we!?"

"Say it loud and clear, my brother – I could have done so in Freetown", Emmanuel, a soldier from Sierra Leone, commented.

"I am not a Christian, but I think your Holy Book says something like 'leave the dead to bury their dead'?" Babatunde inquired.

"Well well, I think you have quoted out of context", Emmanuel remarked.

"Why out of context? Leave the dead to bury the dead; leave the Indians to bury their Indians, point taken – period!" Kojo Mensah, a soldier from the Gold Coast who was following the discussion, added.

Everyone burst into laughter.

A short period of silence followed.

"Men, be serious", Babatunde broke the silence. "Why don't the beggars on the street, some of whom look physically okay, not leave the city for their respective villages to till the land?"

"I have also been pondering over the matter", Kakra joined in the conversation.

"Well, maybe they are of a lower caste, with no access to the land", Emmanuel conjectured.

"This caste system! The other day, one Indian soldier attempted to explain it to me, but I just could not comprehend it; or maybe I did not want to understand!" Babatunde stated.

"You may be right Emmanuel", Kakra remarked. "Maybe the beggars on the street belong to the lowest possible caste, with no right to land ownership."

"In that case, they can go back to their villages and work as labourers for the land owners instead of staying on the street and risk dying of starvation!" Babatunde suggested.

"My brother, do you think people can die of starvation in our respective countries?" Emmanuel queried.

"Well, I can only speak for the Gold Coast", Kojo Mensah stated. "In the absence of a prolonged drought or a war or unforeseeable natural disaster, I cannot imagine something of this nature happening in the Gold Coast."

"Well, in life never say never", Kakra observed.

"Indeed you are right", Emmanuel agreed.

Chapter 25
Inching slowly but surely towards the battlefield

—*ww*—

F inally, on a warm and bright day in December 1943, Kakra's Division boarded several troopships on the banks of the Hooghly River, a tributary of the Ganges River, and sailed eastwards, heading for the India–Burma border. Their final destination was Chittagong, which is approximately 560 kilometres to the East of Calcutta, travelling by road. After sailing for several hours, the troopships finally docked at the port of Chittagong.

From Chittagong they marched on through the waterlogged and marshy fields of the Bengali countryside, passing through isolated and tiny settlements until they came to a railway station in an isolated location.

"Men, we are going to continue our journey by train", their captain told them. About half an hour after their arrival, a steam engine at the head of a row of carriages appeared on the horizon. It pulled to a stop at the station. "Get on board, everyone!" the announcement came through a megaphone.

After a journey that lasted about an hour, the train pulled to a stop at Doharzi, a little town about 70 kilometres from where they began their journey. The troops were ordered to disembark.

The journey had not ended yet. Instead they were asked to board waiting buses for their final destination, a military camp on the outskirts of the little town of Chiringa.

The camp, which may well be likened to a bamboo town carved out of the forest, would serve as the headquarters of both the 81st and 82nd

Divisions (another Division made up entirely of West African troops which arrived in Burma later on in the campaign) during the conflict.

Kakra arrived at the camp a few days prior to Christmas 1943.

On Christmas Day, he was served corned beef and potato, followed by pudding made from army biscuits and raisins .

Chapter 26

The bloodsucking leeches of the Burma jungle that won't let go of their victims without a fight

—*mm*—

ABOUT A WEEK after their arrival, at their base, a high ranking officer turned up to address the recruits. Assembled in a makeshift bamboo shed, he spoke to them with the help of a megaphone.

"On behalf of Lieutenant General William Slim, GOC 14th Army, I welcome you to South East Asia!

"I am aware that not every one of you is fluent in the English language. After this meeting, those of you who have understood the message of this meeting should explain, in your respective languages, what I have said to those who did not understand me.

"Your division, the 81st, together with the 82nd, which is expected to arrive here in the near future, will be the two divisions to represent West Africa in the multinational force of the 14th Army. Comprised of about a million, well-trained, well-equipped and highly-dedicated soldiers, the 14th Army, in effect, is an international polyglot force consisting of British, Australians, Canadians, South Africans, Burmese, Chinese, Africans and, chiefly, the Indian Army.

"It may interest you to know that together with the 82nd Division, you guys from West Africa – the Gambia, Sierra Leone, the Gold Coast and Nigeria – are contributing around 90,000 men to the 14th Army.

"I am here today, not only to welcome you, but also to give you a short lecture on Burma, the country you will be heading for in the next few days.

Location:
"I want to touch first on its location. It is sandwiched between India to the west, Thailand and the French Protectorate of Laos to the east, China to the north and northeast, with an uninterrupted coastline of 1,200 miles (1,930 km) along the Bay of Bengal and the Andaman Sea to the south.

"Occupying an area of approximately 261,227 square miles (676,578 square kilometres), it stretches across a distance of about 720 miles (1150Km) from Ledo in the north to Rangoon in the south, and 360 miles (580km) from Akyab in the west to Lashio in the north east, each measured along a straight line.

"Burma's terrain becomes lower from north to south – from mountains and plateaus in the north to plains in the south.

"The country's geographical features can be divided into four categories: highlands in the east, mountains in the west, plains in the central area and coastal in the south west Arakan. As far as you are concerned it is the south-western Arakan region that is of importance – since your main area of engagement will be in the Kaladan valley of the Arakan region.

"The landscape in the Arakan in particular is rugged in several places, on occasions we may literally have to crawl along the terrain to make headway.

Climate:
"Burma is endowed with a tropical monsoon climate displaying three main seasons – hot, rainy and cold.

"The hot season falls between February and May. It becomes intensely hot in most parts of the country with daytime temperatures rising above 40°C (104°F). There is little or no rainfall during this time of the year.

"May to October is the rainy season. It is also the period of the monsoon.

"Talking of the monsoon! I have lived in West Africa for a considerable period of time. I experienced some stormy weather during that period, but nothing compared to the monsoon winds of Burma, my friends. They are cyclonic in nature – so powerful they are capable of tossing even big transport planes around as if they were just sheets of paper!

"The monsoon brings in its wake abundant rain. During the period rainfall can be constant for long periods of time.

"The Cold Season extends from November to February. It can be warm during the day, but turns cool at night with temperatures tumbling to around 20 degrees Celsius. For those of us who grew up in Europe, not cold really. But for residents here as well as individuals like yourselves who are used to high temperatures, it could lead to a great deal of shivering!"

Vegetation:
"Facilitated by the rains and a fertile soil, the vegetation tends to grow at a rapid rate. Jungle roads that are not frequented by traffic can soon become obscured by overgrown bushes.

"Indeed, the vegetation in the Burmese jungle is in some areas virtually impenetrable by virtue of the thick undergrowth.

"Devoid of paths and roads in several places, we will have to cut through the thick jungle to create paths to facilitate our forward march.

Population:
"You also need to have a brief knowledge of the population make-up of the country; such knowledge is vital to our campaign, especially in the area of intelligence gathering.

"Just as in the case of your various countries where several ethnic groups exist side by side, Burma is also a multiethnic, multilingual, and multicultural society.

"The Burman form the majority, with the Shan, the Karen, the Arakanese (Rakhine) and the Mon following in a reducing order of population size.

"As I just mentioned, the Burman ethnic group, who speak the Burmese language, is the largest and culturally dominant ethnic group in Burma. They inhabit the central plains of the country including the cities of Rangoon and Mandalay. Theravada Buddhism is a major aspect of the Burman culture and nearly all Burman people are Buddhists.

"The Karen constitute the second largest ethnic group. Prior to the arrival of the Europeans, they ascribed to an animist faith. With the advent of the Christian missionaries, some converted to Christianity.

"There has been a long standing animosity between the Burmans and the Karens. I do not want to go into details in this regard, but for the sake of our impending operation, I want you only to keep in mind that the British rule was favourably accepted by the Karens.

"Having provided a brief background of the population of Burma, I want you to know that not every Burmese is against the occupation of their country.

"Basically, the Burmese Buddhists who make up the majority of the population look favourably on the Japanese, who also share their faith. Some indeed rejoiced at the arrival of the Japanese, in January 1942, with chants of 'Asia for the Asians!' We have to be cautious with our dealings with them – they are likely to supply intelligence to the enemy in regard to our movements.

"On the other end of the spectrum are the Burmese Muslims, and other ethnic minorities such as the Karens, Kachins and Chins, who feel a greater allegiance towards the British. As might be expected, they are likely to assist us in our endeavours.

"A population group that cannot be overlooked are the Indian immigrants. Their number is estimated to be around a million. They view the English more favourably and would be more inclined to assist us, including providing useful intelligence about the enemy, for example.

"Also of particular importance for you in view of the fact that you will be mainly engaged in the Arakan are the Kumis, the local tribesmen of the Kaladan Valley.

"Prior to the invasion of Burma by the Japanese, they lived in relative isolation in the Kaladan Valley, engaged in small-scale rice farming and also fishing.

"The Japanese invasion has now brought them in the limelight. We must go to great lengths to court their friendship because they could be of enormous assistance to us in our reconnaissance and espionage activities.

Other matters:

"Having provided you with an overview of the geography and population make-up of the country, I want to draw your attention to other very important issues.

"We face a formidable foe in the form of the highly motivated Japanese Army. As if the opposition we face from the declared enemy was not enough, the hot and humid climate combined with the abundant rainfall, has facilitated not only the burgeoning or thriving growth of the vegetation, but also has provided a conducive environment for the thriving of various types and kinds of life – insects, parasites, bacteria, you can go on naming them.

"Some of the organisms carry serious diseases such as malaria, tropical sprue, dengue fever, dysentery, cholera, etc., on their own or may serve as vectors for their spread.

"We are taking appropriate measures aimed at disease prevention.

"In the case of malaria, you will be supplied with a yellow-coloured pill with the name of Atabrine. I want to encourage everyone to take it as prescribed. Take it from me, it is an effective prophylaxis against the deadly disease.

"Unfortunately, it has come to the attention of the leadership that many a soldier has developed an antipathy towards the tablet on the grounds that it is bitter, that it imparts its yellow hue to the skin after taking it and that it produces unpleasant side-effects like headache, nausea, and vomiting.

"Much as I cannot wholly discard such claims, weighing the disadvantages against the advantages, I will strongly urge everyone to take it as directed – unless of course you want to be sent to your untimely death by the cursed plasmodium parasite. I personally would prefer to die the death of a gallant soldier, by way for example of enemy bullets, than be knocked out by a microscopic parasite, whatever form or shape it may take!

"Notwithstanding your own personal preferences, you are here at the orders of King and Empire. We need your contribution in the arduous task ahead, so make sure you take those bloody pills as advised!

"I am afraid, if we get the impression you are either not taking them or not doing so regularly, we will introduce steps aimed at ensuring you are complying with the rules. In one of the units I visited recently, medics and/or NCOs were positioned at the food collection points to closely watch the men swallow down the tablets handed them with their meals. I hope you will not force your commanders to resort to such measures.

"You should also beware of the leeches – the damn blood-sucking worms! I assume they do exist in West Africa as well. Well, they certainly abound in the jungles of Burma. When they get at you, they bore into your flesh and can be up to an inch deep! They won't let go of you without a fight. Indeed, the only thing that will force them to release their hold on their host is the burning sensation as a result of a lighted cigarette applied to their bodies!

"Oh! I nearly forgot to mention the bugs and ticks. Indeed, not only will the leeches seek to make life in the jungle unpleasant for you, the bugs and ticks will as well.

"I am sure you are not scared as a result of the challenges I have just touched upon. Many of you have survived the equally harsh living conditions in West Africa, so you will surely do the same in the Burma jungle.

"Finally, I wish you all the best of everything. May your stay in South East Asia broaden your horizons and empower you to face any life challenges that will confront you long after you have put this tour of duty behind you and returned to your various countries."

Chapter 27
The Burma–West African highway

~~~

A FEW DAYS AFTER the welcome speech of the representative of the General Officer Commanding, the troops were asked, after a tough day's training session, to gather at the assembly point for yet another address, this time by one of the leading officers of their division.

After everyone had been called to order, the officer began to address them:

"Brave Soldiers of the 81st Division, give me your attention", he began.

Absolute silence prevailed in the assembly as all eyes were directed at him.

"It is superfluous to mention here that every one of you is aware why you are here. Just by way of a reminder, I want to stress the fact that we are here to confront the intransigent Japanese; not only that, but also to rout them out, to make it clear to them it doesn't pay to go about invading the territories of other countries.

"Before I go on to state the specific role you will play, I want to provide you with a short background account in regard to the genesis of the conflict. For some of you it may come as a repetition; for the sake of those who are not as informed as yourselves, I ask you to bear with me.

"In the middle of January 1942 Japan invaded Burma from Thailand. You may want to know what led them to that unprovoked act? Two reasons have been cited.

1) Japan at that time was occupying China. The Nationalist China army which was resisting the Japanese occupation was receiving a steady

stream of military aid from the British. The aid was being transported from the Burmese capital Rangoon, along the Burma Road, the main land route leading from Burma to China. By invading Burma and taking control of the Burma Road, Japan sought to cut the important supply route to the Chinese opposition.

2) The invasion was part of the strategy of the so-called Axis powers – Germany, Italy and Japan – to expand their territories through military conquest. Taking control of Burma would further that cause by placing the Japanese at the gate of India, where they believed general insurrection against the British presence in the vast territory of India would be ignited. That could eventually lead Britain to lose control of their vast Asian colony; Japan could then capitalise on the situation and take control of India. You may call it wishful thinking; I have no doubt in my mind that the Japanese entertained that scenario at the back of their minds.

"Initially, the Japanese scored remarkable successes in their endeavour; in March 1942, Rangoon, the Burmese capital, fell to them.

"After the initial setbacks, British and Indian forces regrouped and attempted to dislodge the invaders. The Japanese invaders, who in the meantime had set up well-prepared defensive positions, easily warded off the British Indian Offensive. In May 1942, the Allies were forced to retreat from Burma into India, accompanied by thousands of refugees who had to endure untold suffering, many dying in the process. Well, the Japanese occupation has persisted to this day; otherwise, you wouldn't be here!" He paused for a while to take a look at his men. From the look of their faces, every one of them appeared to be following his speech very attentively.

He continued after a momentary interlude:

"As far as we are concerned, our area of operation will be mainly in and around the valley of the River Kaladan in the Arakan region. The Arakan is a narrow strip of land, about 400 miles in length and lies sandwiched between the Bay of Bengal and the west of the country. It is cut off from the rest of the country by a range of mountains, by the name of Arakan Yoma.

"In the south, the territory is made up of open and largely flat paddy fields, mangrove swamps and wide rivers which flow in winding loops akin to the movement of snakes.

"Whereas the south is flat and swampy, the north consists of mountains and dense jungles – jungles so thick that even on a bright sunny day, with the sun high in the sky, one would require a torch to find one's way in the gloom resulting from the thick canopy of leaves and branches that prevents hardly any ray of light from penetrating through to the ground.

"The main bulk of our Division will be assigned the task of supporting the Indian XV Corps, an infantry division of the British India Army, in the task of dislodging the Japanese from their strongholds of the Kaladan valley.

"A small fraction of our Division will be attached to the Chindits. For the sake of those who will be in that group, it is worth noting that the Chindits is a special force within our proud army trained to carry out surprise attacks behind the lines of the Japanese foe. The duty of those of you who will be assigned to them will be to guard and defend their bases against possible enemy incursions whilst they are away on their guerrilla-like attacks against the adversary."

He paused for a while to cast his glance around. Just as in the case of Kakra, each one of the men remained still and focussed. Kakra put on a brave face, not wanting to betray the heightened anxiety that was going through him. He was days away from the battlefield, it was clear to him. Would he come out alive? Would he ever see again the face of Panin and other members of his family? If he should succumb to the assailants' bullets, would his body be retrieved and given a decent burial?

Their superior continued his address after the short interlude.

"So men, we are about to begin the march into the Arakan. Before us lies thick, thick jungle. There are no roads, not even jungle paths, along which we can drive our vehicles to transport both our material supplies as well as our troops. We need to construct a road from scratch. We have no machinery to help us – indeed, we don't!

"What we have are basic tools and instruments – picks, shovels, machetes, explosives, etc., and more importantly, strong, well-built and highly motivated men ready to labour and shed their sweat to make this happen.

"Men, are we ready for the task? If so, shout yeah after me!"

"Yeah!"

"Yeah!" the yells of the men filled the air.

"Yeah!"

"Yeah!"

"Yeah!"

"Y-a-a- a- a -a -a-h!" the men screamed all together.

"I am really impressed by your motivation, enthusiasm and sense of duty", the officer said. "So, get ready for action! Starting from early tomorrow work will begin on the construction of our 'Jungle Highway'!"

As ordered by the senior officer, the soldiers went into action the next day to construct the announced access road. Starting from their Indian base at Chiringa, they went into action to construct a road through the jungle across the Indian–Burma frontier, right up to the Burmese town Satpaung on the banks of the Kaladan River. At the same time as the troops laboured with their picks and shovels, they all the time remained alert, ready to fight at any moment. For even as they laboured, the Japanese were attempting to make incursions with the goal not only to inflict casualty but also disrupt their progress.

After several weeks of hard work involving among other things, cutting through seemingly impenetrable jungle, hills, huge rocks, etc., the jungle road stretching over 75 miles (120 km) was completed. The West Africans aptly christened the "highway" created through their sweat and labour "the West Africa Way".

No less a figure than the General Officer Commander of the 81st Division, General Woolner, was on site to commission it personally.

Chapter 28

The unique army that conveys its entire jungle supplies through sheer manpower

—mm—

A few days after the commissioning of the "West African Way", the 81st Division got ready to march into Burma.

The plan was to move artillery guns, jeeps and other supplies including of course the troops themselves up to the Burmese town Saptuang on the banks of the Kaladan River. From there the men and ammunition would be transported further across the river in barges and flatboats.

Just before he gave the marching order, the Division commander called them together to give them final instructions:

"I hope you are prepared physically and mentally for the task ahead.

"The entire journey of over a hundred miles will be done on foot. Everything needed for your survival, your food, your clothes, everything, must be transported by yourselves on your heads and backs as the case may be.

"Remember, we are doing all this in the pursuit of freedom, our freedom and the freedom of generations yet unborn.

"We have a formidable enemy to contend with. Yes, indeed, beware of the Japanese soldier! He is certainly a formidable foe – not lacking in bravery, determination, commitment and a sense of duty.

"Indeed if there is one area where the Japanese soldiers are excellently trained and prepared, it is in the art of jungle warfare. They have mastered the art of concealment in the jungle to perfection. One may well liken him to a snake! Like a serpent, he is capable of crawling under the thick undergrowth for considerable distances with the goal of launching a surprise attack on the enemy.

"Furthermore, they are excellent tricksters. For example, a single soldier might tie two machine guns each to two neighbouring trees and attach a long chord to the trigger of each of the guns. Holding on firmly to the two ends of the chord, he can lie concealed in the undergrowth in wait for the enemy. On spotting the enemy approaching, he will pull on the chords and unleash the fire power of the guns against them and at the same time throw grenades at them. Though coming from one individual, the impression on the enemy will be firepower from several attackers!

"By virtue of having arrived here before ourselves, they have the advantage of having become more familiar with this hostile environment. Nevertheless, I am sure we shall catch up in no time!

"As you will expect, the Japanese would like to exploit their better knowledge of the terrain to their advantage. They could conceal themselves at strategic locations and launch surprise attacks against us. Of course, this is a conflict and I do not guarantee that we can pre-empt every planned ambush of the enemy.

"We should indeed be very weary of ambushes from a fanatical enemy who would prefer to die than to be taken prisoner.

"Indeed, our intelligence tells us that the Japanese soldiers have been brainwashed to believe that there is a place in the Japanese heaven reserved for any soldier killed defending the land of their ancestors. Of course, this battle is not fought on the land of their ancestors, but they will nevertheless go all the way to defend it.

"If anyone is captured, under no circumstance should that individual provide the enemy information concerning troop movement, nor the identity of the unit. Indeed you should not go beyond supplying anything other than your name, rank and service number if required. I know this will not be relevant to our West African comrades. Still, I want to announce to you as well, as I do to all units: whoever is keeping a diary, letter or photograph, no matter who is depicted on the photo –

self, spouse, parent (s) – should hand them over. They will be kept safe and handed back to you at the end of the conflict."

And so the march into Burma, to attempt to dislodge the Japanese from their jungle strongholds, got underway.

Chapter 29
An eccentric resident of a small African town's free counsel to the powers that be

~~~

TWO DAYS AFTER leaving the Chiringa camp, the troops reached Saptuang on the banks of the Kaladan River. From there the men and ammunition were transported further across the river in barges and flatboats. Finally, the march from the banks of the Kaladan River into the heartlands of the Arakan got underway. The information had been spread around that the plan was for them to march about 80 miles from the starting point onto a plain overlooking some mountain ranges. A jungle camp was to be established there. From there the plan was to carry out guerrilla-like raids against the enemy camped a distance of about five miles behind the said mountain ranges.

There was nothing by way of a road or even a path in sight. Just as in the matter of the West African Way, the troops would have to cut a passage through the jungle to facilitate their movement – with the important exception that it did not need to be a broad road, but just wide enough to permit human movement.

So, they went to work; armed with machetes; they set about to cut through thick jungle undergrowth to clear the way needed for their forward movement. Progress was slow; on some days they managed to create only a few hundred metres of pathway.

In that manner, they, day by day, slowly but steadily moved forward through the thick jungle, along rugged terrain, over rocks; and so, up and down hills, hillocks and mountain ranges, across valleys, they advanced.

On some occasions, they had to wade through streams and rivers, where the water rose above the waist, indeed at times just below nose level, and often not for short distances; indeed, in some cases they had to wade distances exceeding a mile along the course of rivers that abounded in the area.

Leaving the river behind, their path could take them along stretches of marshy, waterlogged ground. As they inched their way along the muddy terrain, slipping and falling became the lot of the wearied soldiers.

As they struggled to make progress through the thick jungle, thick drops of sweat dripped from Kakra's forehead due to the scorching heat. His neck felt it would break under the weighty burden on his head, his back hurting from the heavily laden rucksack strapped to it. His heavy legs were hardily able to respond to the signals from his brain to keep on going, his parched lips reminding him of the thirst that was building up in him. Last but not least, the hunger pangs were beginning to set in, and he yearned for the relieving signal from their captain to cease moving and rest awhile.

As if the physical agony he was experiencing was not enough, from time to time vexatious thoughts, indeed irritating thoughts that centred on the purpose of the whole undertaking went through his mind, threatening to send him *stark raving mad.*

What indeed was all the fuss about? Why were they engaged in this seemingly senseless and gruelling expedition in the first place?

Of course, they had been told that they were there to end the Japanese occupation of Burma. And he would not indeed dispute the fact that the Japanese had indeed invaded the country.

The British, on their part, more concerned about losing India, their huge Asian colony, were, as might be expected, bent on resisting the Japanese aggressor with tooth and nail.

As far as Kakra was concerned, that did not adequately answer the question as to why they were there – the Japanese, on the one hand and, on the other, the Africans who had been ferried over 10,000 kilometres to confront them. Why, from a philosophical point of view, were they assembled in the jungle, disturbing the peace of the indigenous population the likes of the Kumis together with the wildlife – Burmese tigers, monkeys, cobras, pythons, mosquitoes, etc.? What was it all about?

In such moments, his thoughts would go back to his native Kojokrom, to Kwaasuo, one of the residents there. Whether he was still alive, he could not tell. He knew that up to the time of that fateful day when they left for the hunting expedition he was alive; not only alive, but fit as a fiddle. In any case, his imagination ran rife through this type of thinking, and his mind went back to a time when he and his brother Panin met Kwaasuo on the streets of their little settlement.

"What are you two nasty fellows doing on the street at this time of the night?" Kwaasuo demanded.

"What have we done to you to warrant the description 'nasty'?" Panin queried.

"You shut up, or you will get a slap on the face!" Kwaasuo said, jumping towards them. Sensing danger both boys took to their heels and ran away as fast as they could.

Kwaasuo's behaviour was so bizarre and his thoughts so illogical that most of the time everyone in the little community took him for someone who was not in control of his mental faculties – indeed he had the reputation of being as nutty as a fruitcake! He on the other hand saw things in a different light, considering everyone else, apart from himself, as crazy! One of his popular sayings was: "This is mine, that is mine, and at the end of the day we are all food for worms!"

If the powers that be could learn sense from this "crazy-minded" loner of little Kojokrom, and be satisfied with what was theirs and not seek to occupy lands, indeed encroach on other people's territories, many a conflict raging in the world – in Africa, Europe, Asia and elsewhere – would not have been fought in the first place. Or so Kakra surmised.

Until that happened, however, the ordinary players in the conflict, the Japanese and Empire soldiers, individuals who may well have been good friends had they chanced to meet on the streets of Tokyo, London, Banjul, Sokoto, etc., prior to the outbreak of the conflict, had no option than to fight each other – indeed to aim a gun at each other in accordance with the bitter, but unavoidable, battlefield reality: "Either I eliminate the enemy first or the enemy eliminates me!"

Chapter 30
Bone-breaking techniques of infrastructural development in the Burmese jungle

~~~

After covering a distance of about 75 miles on foot, the unit commander gave the order for everyone to stop marching and pay attention:

"Our unit is going to set up camp here. I have received intelligence to the effect that the enemy is camped behind a range of mountains not very far from here. So, as I said, we are going to set up camp here. From time to time we shall despatch small units to launch surprise attacks against the enemy. So let us get going, men!"

Soon they got down to work. Making use of machetes, they first cleared the thick undergrowth. Next, with the same machetes, they felled the trees, some of which had attained considerable sizes. The task of felling the trees was carried out in turns; after one soldier had been on the job for about half an hour, he was relieved by another.

When it came to the turn of Kakra, he cast his mind back to the time he was growing up at Kojokrom. After Duku had cleared the thick undergrowth of a portion of virgin forest meant for the cultivation of food crops in a particular year, he set about, with the help of an axe, to fell the large trees growing on the farmland before planting was carried out. Kakra could at that time only wonder how he managed to achieve that feat. Now he was called upon to participate in something similar, yet even more challenging.

After several days of bone-breaking work, which involved the shedding of considerable sweat from the highly motivated soldiers, the jungle camp was ready.

A few days after the completion of work on the jungle camp, their battalion leader gathered them around himself and began:

"Men, as you are already aware, there is neither a road nor a railway network far and wide. As a result we will receive our supplies by way of parachuted drops from the air. To be able to evacuate our injured and seriously ill for treatment in our field hospital several miles away, we also need to construct air fields in the jungle.

"How do we go about that without any machinery to assist us? Well, in the same way that you managed, with your physical strength and the few tools at your disposal, to construct the West Africa Way. I am calling on you to use the same means to construct an air field at this very place."

The unit commander then, with a stern look, singled out one of the men, addressing him directly.

"Yemi", he said, "we are capable of the task, aren't we?"

"*Olourun!*" the man responded nervously, clearly taken aback by suddenly becoming the focal point of everyone's attention. He pointed to the heavens.

"What do you mean by *Olouron?*" the group leader inquired.

"*Olourun* means 'God of the Heavens' in the Yoruba language!" someone explained.

"What has God to do in this matter?"

"I believe we shall succeed with God's help", Yemi said.

"Well, I am not a religious man", the unit commander said. "I used to accompany my parents to church as a child but have never stepped into church as an adult. Still, I do remember one of the passages I heard from Sunday school: 'Render unto Caesar what is Caesar's, and to God what is God's.'

"Well based on my own interpretation of that verse of Scripture, Yemi, you can pray at home on your own – in that way you can '*Render to God what is God's!*'

"But the assignment before us, as far as I am concerned, has nothing to do with God. It has to do with Caesar if you like. So Yoruba-speaking soldier from… from…?"

"Nigeria!" Yemi helped him out.

"Thank you. Well, my Yoruba friend from Nigeria, the assignment before us is Caesar's, so we are going to give unto Caesar what is Caesar's by using our human power in the construction of the required airfield rather than rely on any superhuman sources to help us sort it out. So men, one, two, three, let's get ready to work!"

At this point Kakra had an idea that would help the men to work together, in a concerted effort.

"May I teach the men a Gold Coast work song?" he inquired.

"Nothing religious?" the head of the unit queried.

"No, just a rhythmic song of a few lines, with practically no meaning; just to provide the needed boost."

"Okay, go ahead."

"It goes like this:

"When I cry out 'T-s-c-h-o-o-b-o-y-e!!' the rest must respond with a cry of 'Y-e-e-e-i!'

"So here we go: 1, 2, 3….

"T-s-c-h-o-o-b-o-y-e!!"

"Y-e-e-e-i!" the contingent yelled in reply.

"T-s-c-h-o-o-b-o-y-e!!"

"Y-e-e-e-i!"

"T-s-c-h-o-o-b-o-y-e!!"

"Y-e-e-e-i!"

Soon the men got down to work. With the help of their machete, they cleared first the undergrowth. Next, they used the same tools to fell not only the trees growing directly on the field but also those growing in the neighbourhood deemed to be standing within falling distance from the perimeters of the field.

After several days of hard labour the airfield was completed. It would be the first of its kind to be built in the manner just described. In the course of the campaign soldiers of the 81st Division were called upon to construct several other airstrips.

As Kakra learnt towards the end of the campaign, in all a total of 25 light aircraft and 11 transport aircraft landing strips were constructed in the manner just described during the campaign.

Chapter 31
Arakan daily news bulletin

～mm～

K AKRA'S TOUR OF DUTY in the Arakan region of Burma lasted from the middle of January 1944 till towards the end of January 1945. A great deal happened during the 12-month period. A detailed account of his day-to-day experiences would require a few volumes of books if not several to record. Only a brief outline of the day-to-day living experiences in the jungle camps, some of the striking encounters, and the major military campaigns involving in particular his 81st Division as well as the 82nd (the other West African division in the conflict) and the 14th Army in general during the period, will be provided in this account.

MAP OF BURMA

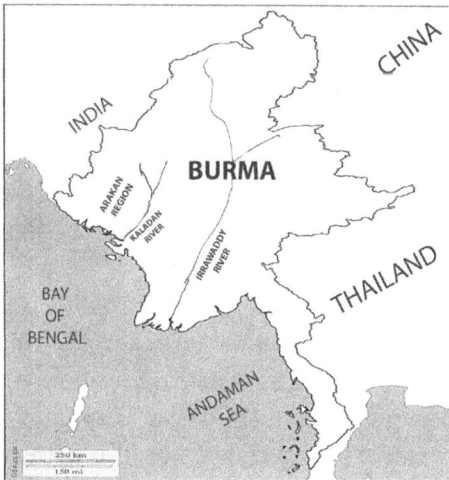

- **Monkey Meat Palaver**

What could be a more appropriate way to begin an account of the day-to-day living experiences of the soldiers pitched in the thick Burmese jungle other than to touch on the matter that was basic for their survival, namely their food supply?

As mentioned earlier, supplies came mainly in the form of air drops. When the men were in their jungle bases, one could count on regular meals. On the other hand, if they happened to be on the move, there was not always a guarantee that the "iron rations" they carried in their rucksacks – tins of corned beef, canned sardines, pieces of fruit as well as chocolate, biscuits, jam and tea – would be enough to see them through to the accomplishment of their specific assignments. Indeed on not a few occasions food became scarce, to the point that made the soldiers feel the real threat of starvation.

Though Kakra only rarely engaged in such deeds, on some occasions, nevertheless, he and his fellow soldiers were forced, as it were, to reap what they had not sown, i.e. on the farms of the indigenous jungle dwellers – in defiance, in effect, of their military code of conduct.

When the farm owners happened to see them, coming across them red handed, as it were, a reverse situation to what one would usually expect to happen when someone catches a thief on his or her property transpired! Instead of confronting the "thieves" and reprimanding them for their bad behaviour, they, out of fear for the armed soldiers, took to their heels and ran away as far as their legs could carry them.

Apart from this illicit means of food acquisition, occasionally they made use of their guns to hunt some of the wildlife roaming the jungle. Though this was frowned upon by their commanders, especially in view of the risk of drawing the attention of the enemy to their presence by the sound of gunshot, whenever they ran desperately short of food supplies they were tempted to disregard the rule.

Kakra recalled not a few instances when they elatedly feasted on the meat of some of the monkeys that abounded in the jungle. Apart from the Sierra Leonean soldiers, all the West Africans enjoyed the opportunity.

"My God, how can anyone think of eating monkey meat!" their Sierra Leonean friends and comrades would taunt them.

"It tastes really good!" they would reply.

"Eh, that's distasteful – eating the flesh of beings that looks like ourselves!"

"Well, as the saying has it: 'One man's food is another man's poison'."

"I'm aware of a different version of the saying", one of the soldiers joined in.

"How does it go?"

"'One man's trash is another man treasure!'"

There was still yet another means by which the troops supplemented their food supplies, namely by way of fishing in the streams and rivers. Their method was in no way conventional; it was namely by way of throwing grenades into the rivers or streams in order to harvest the fish that perished from the explosion.

- **Water insecurity in the midst of plenty**

As mentioned earlier on, monsoon winds brought abundant rain. The rains on their part fed several streams and rivers. While water was therefore in abundance, it was not free from disease-bringing micro-organisms.

To reduce the risk of water-borne disease, the troops were supplied with chlorine tablets to treat their drinking water.

Apart from the threat posed to their water by microscopic organisms, the Japanese enemy on not a few occasions endangered their water supply by poisoning it.

Kakra spoke about one particular instance when the enemy brought his unit into grave danger by poisoning all the streams and rivers in the vicinity of their camp. For several days following the malicious disruption of their water supply, each soldier was forced to rely on a single bottle of drinking water.

- **Jungle hygiene**

Kakra deemed it superfluous to mention the fact that there were no toilets in the jungle; they had to make do with makeshift dug-out lavatories built by their own labour in their various jungle camps.

In the matter of washing themselves and their clothes, they resorted to several of the rivers and streams (known as *chaungs* by the indigenous population). The rivers and *chaungs* indeed, abound in the area, and it is superfluous to mention that the recruits usually set up camps near them. They had to be on the watch out for ambushes from the enemy as they bathed in the rivers and streams. As a precaution, some of them kept guard, with loaded guns ready to be fired at whoever dared attack them.

- **Havoc of death-bringing snakes**

The soldiers had to be aware not only of wild beasts such as tigers and striped hyenas that abound in the jungle, but also snakes! Some of the snakes, though small in size, were nevertheless very venomous. On rare occasions some, somehow, managed to crawl up the trousers of the unsuspecting soldiers to inflict fatal bites.

Initially the recruits slept on blankets spread on the bare jungle floor. Soon this method was abandoned. Instead, sleeping platforms rising a few centimetres above the ground were constructed for this purpose – to keep the men dry and safe from the many insects and snakes common in the jungle.

Chapter 32
Ubiquitous death angels of the Burmese jungle

—*mm*—

S OON THE DIFFERENCE between the East African campaign and that of the Burma jungle dawned on Kakra.

The most striking difference was that, unlike the East African campaign, in the jungle campaign the battle lines were not clearly drawn, if one could even consider them as battle lines at all.

The reality was that the enemy hid themselves, concealed in thick, barely penetrable jungle, and were capable of firing on them at any moment. As a result of this, whenever Kakra and his unit moved, they reckoned with threats and dangers that could befall them at any time – an ambush, where enemy soldiers could pounce on them from any direction, bullets targeting them from any possible direction, explosives thrown at them, from who knows where!

In the course of time Kakra and his mates became wary of two types of sound. The first was the sound of *ka-ka-ka* – emanating from the machine guns of the enemy hiding somewhere in the thick jungle. The other sound was a whistling noise from explosives directed at them by the enemy, who could be hiding behind a tree, or any suitable object that might conceal them.

Chapter 33
The 'seeing is believing' attitude of an English mate

~~~

As Kakra found out, with the exception of himself and a few others, a good many of the African soldiers carried objects such as a talisman, effigies of their fetish beliefs, rings, etc., to the battlefields, both in East Africa and Burma in the belief that these would offer them protection from harm.

One day as Kakra and a group of African soldiers accompanied by three of their British mates went to have a bath in a stream, the exposure of the objects worn around the waists and necks of some of the Africans led Peter, one of the British mates, to put the question:

"Why are you wearing such items?"

"Without my talisman I would be dead", Musah, a Nigerian soldier replied.

"Really?"

"Well, I have already on a few occasions escaped death – thanks to my amulet."

"Hmm!" Peter sighed, clearly not convinced.

"Well, I know you may find it hard to believe", Musah said, "but it is a fact. I have indeed on several occasions been preserved from harm by my devoted protector guardian. I will cite only one example. During my tour of duty in East Africa, my unit unexpectedly came under air bombardment from the Italian Air Force. The attack came unexpectedly and many of us could not make it into our defensive shelters in time. In the event we lost almost half of the unit; those who remained suffered various injuries, from light to life-threatening. Thanks to my amulet, however, I was the only one who escaped unharmed."

"I don't believe that damn thing could save you!" Robert, one of the English soldiers, stated. "It was luck, mere luck that kept you from harm!"

"I know you Europeans don't believe in such things, but I tell you they work!"

"It's not only our European mates who have their doubts", Kakra said, joining the discussion. "I do not believe in such powers as well."

"Hey, my friend, you are from Africa and you don't believe in Juju?"

"I believe in Almighty God!"

"Well, I also believe in Almighty God; in my opinion belief in God should not exclude belief in juju, charms, magic, etc. The belief in the existence of God should, in my opinion, serve to underpin the idea that superhuman forces – juju, charms, magic, etc., are a reality. God is the Big Boss, the Major Force of the universes; juju, charms, magic, are lesser forces that can still offer human protection."

"Well, I prefer to stick with the Big Boss, rather than have anything to do with your lesser gods", Kakra asserted.

"Well, I side with Musah in the matter", Kamara, a soldier from Sierra Leone, said as he joined in the discussion. "You may find what I am about to narrate hard to believe. Well, initially I also did not believe it. But it has been corroborated by so many different soldiers that I really find it difficult to discredit it. There is one NCO in our battalion. I think he is a Mossi-speaking man from the Gold Coast. He is credited with extraordinary powers – to the extent that every infantry man wants to be in his unit."

"Indeed?" Musah interposed.

"Yes."

"What can he do?"

"He is credited with the ability to move soldiers away from danger."

"What do you mean by that?" Robert asked, somewhat surprised.

"Well, according to the troops that have fought alongside him, whenever they found themselves in a dangerous situation, he summoned the help of an amulet he was wearing to whisk them out of the scene of danger, which happened instantly!!"

"Stop it, stop it!" Peter yelled. "This is too much for me to bear!"

"Then you better shut both of your ears, my doubting European friend!" Kamara yelled back. Everyone present burst into laughter.

Kamara continued after a short while.

"Yes indeed, his magical powers were able to whisk himself and everyone present from danger. No one could explain how it happened; the fact is whenever he appealed to his amulet, he and members of his unit were transported by an unseen hand away from the scene of danger to a safe place!!"

"How can you believe such a fantasy, Kamara!" Robert exclaimed.

"Well, as I made it clear at the outset, I heard the story not from only one source but several others."

"My question is, have you experienced it yourself?"

"No; the reason being that I have never served in his unit!"

Just at that moment, Komla Sefadzi, an Ewe-speaking soldier from the Gold Coast, pulled an amulet from his pocket and began:

"I initially did not want to take part in this discussion. I feel in the meantime compelled to do so, indeed to let the sceptics among us know that there are indeed unseen forces operating in the universe.

"I want everyone here to take a look at this talisman." As he spoke he raised the brown round object in his hand so everyone present could have a look. "It was given to me by a fetish I consulted in my village prior to embarking on this tour of duty. It is my bullet-proof protector! So long as I keep to some set rules, I cannot be injured by a bullet, even if I am fired upon at short range!"

"What rules?" Peter wanted to know.

"That is a secret! The moment I let it out of the bag, it will lose its protecting powers."

"So, you really believe in it?" Kakra wanted to know.

"Of course; it has already protected me on several occasions. Indeed, I wouldn't be alive today without its shielding powers."

"Okay, my friend", Peter said. "I do not want to argue with you. I only want proof. So, without further ado, you stand a few metres away from me whilst I fetch my rifle and I aim a few shots at you. We shall see whether that damned charm can indeed protect you!"

"You surely have no idea how such charms work! A vital mode of operandi is for the bearer or wearer as the case may be not to provoke it into action in the manner you have just suggested. That would be tantamount to a show off. The charm would not offer protection in such a contrived situation. It only unleashes its protecting capabilities when the bearer is exposed to danger in a real-life situation, for example when he or she is fired on in the battlefield!"

"Well, I don't think I can ever be made to believe in these alleged supernatural powers." Robert shook his head. "We came here however to have a bathe in the refreshing waters of the Kaladan! So men, one two three, come along and let's refresh ourselves!" Saying that, Robert took a leap into the river – to be followed moments later by all the others.

Chapter 34
Colour-swapping tactics of scared soldiers

—*mm*—

O ne day a small reconnaissance unit made up of 5 African soldiers including Kakra and their British captain were sent on an intelligence-gathering mission in regard to the troop movement activities of the enemy.

Just as they took a bend, the commander spotted, with the help of his binoculars, a contingent of enemy troops numbering about two dozen walking along the same bush path they were treading and heading towards them!

"Men, quick, let's take cover in the undergrowth!" the group leader commanded his men.

They lay side by side. The captain pulled a small container from his pocket, opened it, poured part of the contents, a black liquid, into in his palm and began to rub it onto his face and both arms not covered by his green military short-sleeved uniform.

"I need to look like you guys", he whispered into the ears of Kakra who happened to be lying closest to him. "My light skin colour may otherwise betray me to the enemy!"

"So, you want to be an African?" Kakra whispered back.

"At least as long as the conflict lasts; your skin is the best camouflage against detection."

"Who knows, perhaps your ancestors were Africans after all", Kakra smiled. "They just migrated north of Africa, to Europe. In the course of time their – and your – skin colour just turned light."

"Well, that might well have been the case. For now though let's stop talking – the enemy is only a few steps away."

As everyone lay in silence, Kakra could feel his heart not only pounding, but also racing. Would the Japanese spot them and blow their bodies apart, to be fed upon by the hungry Burmese tigers?

At that juncture, his thoughts went to his boyhood and teenage years, to the nights when he and his peers gathered at the centre of the little settlement to engage in *Akuntun,* the local version of the universal *children's* game of hide-and-seek. One of them was selected to play the hider. As the rest kept their eyes shut, the hider quickly vanished out of sight and hid behind anything that could help conceal the player, indeed that could help prevent detection by the others. After keeping their eyes shut for a short while, the others would go out to "hunt" for the hidden playmate.

No one needed to point out to him that the situation he found himself in the thick jungle of South East Asia, thousands of kilometres away from the fringes of his little town, was far from a children's game of hide-and-seek – for indeed it bordered on life and death.

Was it triggered probably by the pollen of some of the plants blooming near where they sought refuge? Kakra could only conjecture, but as it happened, just as the Japanese were passing the path close to where they were hiding, indeed only a stone's throw away, all of a sudden, a sneezing sensation began building up in him.

The thought went through him: "I need to suppress this damn thing, or I'll betray not only myself but my comrades as well!"

At that juncture, a tip that one of his unit commanders had given him and his unit several weeks before on how to suppress a sneeze came to mind: "Breathe forcefully through the nose or press on the upper lip below the nose or rub the nose!"

Breathing forcefully through the nose was not the most sensible thing to do in the situation, he reasoned. In the end, he went for the third option. After rubbing his nose several times, the urge rescinded. In the meantime, thank goodness, the enemy had moved on. After remaining in the hideout for several minutes, the order came from the group leader to head back to the jungle base.

Chapter 35
A striking heart under scorching midday heat

—*mm*—

O n another occasion, as they marched on in the scorching midday heat that bit mercilessly on the troops, one of them, complained of a sudden onset of left-sided chest pain.

The commander called a halt to the march and attended to him.

"I am not only experiencing pain", the man said, "I am also feeling dizzy and light headed."

"Put down you load and rest for a while", the commander advised him. Just as the others helped him get the load off his head, he collapsed to the ground and lost consciousness. His comrades attended to him and tried to resuscitate him – to no avail.

Kakra was deeply affected by the loss. The man was a comrade from the Gambia, a man full of humour and goodwill. Adamu, as he was known, that being his first name, had virtually become the unofficial entertainer of the group, keeping their spirits up with a lot of jokes and banter.

What was to be done with his mortal remains? Far removed from their base, carrying him was out of the question.

After pondering the matter for a while, their unit commander instructed the men to quickly dig a grave and dispose of the body until, hopefully, a favourable opportunity would crop up in the future when it could be retrieved.

Soon they went into action to dig a makeshift grave in the jungle. Before they left, the commander marked the spot on his map, promising to ensure the body would be retrieved at a more conducive time.

Chapter 36
The colour bar of a multinational army

—*mm*—

AS MENTIONED EARLIER, the 14th Army, which also came to be referred to as the "Forgotten Army" because the British Empire paid much more attention to its army fighting Nazi Germany on mainland Europe rather than the branch fighting in faraway Asia, was a multinational troop comprised of men from various parts of the Empire, in particular India.

Kakra and his mates soon learnt with indignation the discrimination that was meted out, especially against one group of the multinational and multi-ethnic mix – the West Africans. For example, whereas all private soldiers of the division were black, the officers were white, and came from Europe and white South Africa as well as Rhodesia. Every patrol of the West Africans had to be led by a British non-commissioned officer. The explanation given was that the Africans of Other Ranks (AORs) were insufficiently trained for the job – which the West Africans disputed. Indeed, Kakra identified a few, if not many, sergeants among the West Africans, from Nigeria, who could perform just as well, if not better than the BNCOs.

Without being biased towards them, Kakra and his mates soon realised to their indignation that a good many of the BNCOs set over them were insufficiently trained for the job. Rumours went round among the West Africans to the effect that some of the BNCOs, for various reasons – rude behaviour, incompetence, lack of team spirit, etc. – had been transferred to 81st Division in order that their existing units might be rid of them!

One such BNCO was not only short tempered but also lacking in understanding as to the best way to deal with Africans. In the event he adopted violent tactics bordering on bullying in order to control his men. His attitude was met with resistance from his men – to the point that their resistance threatened to escalate into mutiny. At that point, he was removed from the unit.

One well-educated Nigerian sergeant in Kakra's unit never tired of voicing his disgust at the fact that all British sergeants in the regiment were senior to him, even though he was better educated and could perform better. He kept on complaining about the unfair treatment; in the end, he was transferred to a different platoon. Serving under a non-European platoon commander, he is said to have performed excellently in his new unit.

Chapter 37
The wild rumour mill of the Burmese jungle

—————

S everal wild rumours went round concerning what the Africans were made up of and what they were capable of doing.

Readers will recall Kakra's account of their experience on their arrival in Bombay, how children followed them shouting "Monkeys' tails; monkeys' tails", etc. As a result of the rumour concerning their alleged possession of tails, whenever they went into a river to have a bath, people out of curiosity would come out to stare at them, desirous, as it were, to verify the rumour and to see with their own eyes what the tails of the strange beings looked like!

Yet another fabrication that made its rounds concerned their alleged insatiable appetite for human flesh!

"Place human flesh and beef before them and they will go for the human flesh!" – or so the rumours maintained!

As the Empire Army intelligence soon found out, the Japanese, indeed, believed the lie that associated the African soldiers with cannibalism!

The Empire military commanders saw in these false preconceptions of the enemy towards the African soldiers an opportunity that needed to be seized upon. Soon the Empire Military Command began, actively, to spread the propaganda with the intention of reaching the ears of the Japanese: "The African will be at the forefront of our onslaughts. Be on your guard – they won't only slaughter you, they will devour you alive if you fall into their hands!"

In the midst of the terrible war, a brutal conflict in which the soldiers were exposed to suffering, destruction and death on a regular basis, some of the African soldiers, if only temporarily, lost their sense of humanity and decency.

Though Kakra did not witness it with his own eyes, one of his mates whose credibility he would not dispute told him that on one occasion the unit he was fighting with captured two Japanese soldiers, after they had fatally wounded a couple of them. In the presence of the captured Japanese soldiers, the African soldiers hacked some flesh from the fallen Japanese soldiers and acted as if they were about to devour the hacked-off chunks of meat. At that stage, they set the terribly frightened Japanese free. Scared to death, they took to their heels and ran away, as fast as their legs could carry them!

"Job done!" one of the Africans remarked wryly. "Now they will surely spread the message to their units. 'Beware of the Africans! They will devour your flesh once they capture you'!"

Chapter 38
The woes of the first African player in the premier league division of a renowned army

—*mm*—

ONE DAY there was a pause from active engagement with the enemy due to an involuntary ceasefire imposed by a force beyond the control of the human participants in the conflict – the weather! The *homo sapiens* who seemed incapable of settling conflicts through diplomacy but rather through resorting to naked force, had no choice but to give way to the monsoon rains, which in that particular year hit the area with unusual intensity. Kakra and a few others were consequently relaxing in their jungle camp and engaged in idle banter when one of them raised the issue of commissioned officers in the Empire military establishment and lamented the fact that there was not a single African officer within their ranks.

"I have come across English, Scottish, Welsh, Polish and Indian officers; but I have never come across an African!" he bemoaned.

"Well, then I must correct you on the matter", one of them countered.

"Really?"

"There is one in the 81st Division."

"Really!"

"Yes indeed; Kakra, you must know him."

"Why?" Kakra queried, wondering why Mohammed, the soldier from Kano in Northern Nigeria who had brought up the matter, expected him to be aware of the presence of the said black officer.

"He happens to be from the Gold Coast."

"A Gold Coastian officer in His Majesty's army?"

"Is that what you call residents of the Gold Coast?"

"I have no idea. It is my own invention!"

"Not a bad one."

"Yes, he is from the Gold Coast – a Gold Coastian, or whatever you choose to call one of your fellow citizens!"

"How do you know?"

"Well, on one occasion I served in his unit."

"Well, three cheers for him!"

"Indeed! Anyway, the other day I overheard you people discussing charms and magic, of how some of the troops from Africa came to the battlefield with objects and items they believed would offer them protection from harm. Well, whether he is assisted by supernatural forces or powers, I cannot tell; but the fact remains that he is endowed with extraordinary soldiery qualities which helped him and his unit achieve extraordinary feats on the battlefield.

"One day as I served under him, he led us on a spectacular mission against the enemy. Moving with speed that might well be equated with the speed of lightning, we dashed from behind enemy lines, inflicted heavy casualties on them and, with the speed of a whirlwind, returned to base, casualty-free.

"In the euphoria surrounding the successful outcome of the spectacular mission, our commander, who was otherwise somewhat reserved, opened up to us by telling us something about himself, in particular the circumstances that led to his enlistment in the army and his subsequent commissioning. His goal, he stressed, was not to sing his own praises or blow his horn in front of his men but rather to encourage us to strive for high laurels in life.

"This, in a nutshell, is what Anthony – that's his name – told us:

"Whilst engaged as a teacher at Achimota School in Accra, part of the compound was home to the Headquarters of the Royal West African Frontier Force. He joined the RWAFF in 1939 as a part-time soldier. Later, he applied and was accepted as an officer cadet.

143

"In 1941, he was surprisingly selected by the GOC West African troops for officer training at the Royal Military Academy at Sandhurst in England enrolling there on November 17, 1941."

At that point in his narration one of the men interrupted him with the question:

"How did he fare as the first black officer in training among overwhelmingly white mates?"

"He answered the question with just a single word: perseverance!" Mohammed resumed.

"He went on to explain that his feeling was that racism was an official policy in the army.

He stressed that no less a person than Prime Minister Winston Churchill had come out against commissioning blacks as officers.

He cited an instance when he returned a few minutes late to college from a weekend trip to London. Though he explained that the lateness had been caused by a train delay, he was not excused. Instead he was castigated with the task of clearing snow from the parade ground over a period of fourteen days.

"It was clear to him, the punishment had racial undertones to it, for other whites who found themselves in similar situations were *spared the whip*.

"'Can you imagine a black man, who grew up in the hot climate of Africa, being made to shovel snow in the freezing cold of his first winter?' he put us the question.

"In 1942, he successfully completed his training and attained the rank of Second Lieutenant.

"On his return to the Gold Coast, he was assigned to the 81st Division.

"On his mission to Burma, the troopship he was travelling in, as in the case of Kakra, made a stopover at Durban.

"He took the opportunity of the stopover to make a sight-seeing tour of the city. As he was walking past an open-air bar, he was spotted by some of his white comrades gathered around a table for some chilled beer.

"'Anthony, come over and have a drink', they called out to him on seeing him. He obliged.

"Moments after taking his seat the bar lady came round to serve them.

"'I am not going to serve *him*', she retorted.

"'Why not?'

"The lady remained silent.

"'He is a commissioned officer, serving in His Majesty's army, ready like any one of us to pay the final price for King and Empire!' the officer explained to her.

"'Never mind his military status and capability. The bottom line is that he is a Kaffir[1] and I don't serve Kaffirs!' she stressed, unrepentant."

"How did he react to that?" one of the listeners inquired.

"Well, he put on a brave face and quietly slipped out of the hall."

"That surely must have been hard to swallow!"

"Well, friends, this is what he said: 'I have experienced so many unpleasant things by dint of my skin colour, that I am becoming immune to them. It's really frustrating because, it is not my making that I am endowed with this skin colour.' Anyway, men, you have to keep your heads up in life no matter the obstacles. Like Anthony I urge you to strive to do your best no matter the obstacles. At the end of the day, one can only do one's best and no more than that."

---

[1] A term used in those days in Southern Africa to refer to blacks. Considered today an offensive ethnic slur, in those days it was regarded by whites to be an inoffensive term for black South Africans.

Chapter 39
Two proud empires fight ferociously for control of a strip of jungle land

—*mm*—

HAVING GIVEN THE READER an outline of the day-to-day living experiences in the camp, including some of the striking experiences Kakra underwent, a summary of the main military engagements involving Kakra and the 81st Division in particular and the 14th Army in general during his time in the Burma jungle seems appropriate.

To recap – the main bulk of Kakra's Division was assigned the task of supporting the Indian XV Corps in the task of dislodging the Japanese from their strongholds in and around the Kaladan Valley.

The remainder of the Division was attached to the Chindits.

The main role assigned to the 81st Division attached to the XV Corps was to patrol the jungle of the Arakan region and in so doing protect the left flank of XV Corps from Japanese attack. By protecting the Kaladan Valley and preventing the Japanese from effectively scouting and infiltrating the Arakan, Kakra's Division allowed XV Corps to successfully push the Japanese out of the region. Throughout the period, they engaged in several skirmishes with the Japanese army operating in that area.

Apart from its patrolling role, Kakra's Division was involved in two major operations during the period, namely the second and third Arakan campaigns.

Following the Japanese invasion of Burma, an attempt was made by a combination of British and Indian troops to regain control of the Arakan region from the Japanese invaders. To this end, British and Indian troops engaged the Japanese in a series of skirmishes and battles between December 1942 and April 1943. In the end, the British forces capitulated to the Japanese. This is generally known as the first Arakan campaign.

* Second Arakan campaign

Between February and May 1944, a second attempt at dislodging the Japanese from the Arakan region was undertaken. The attacking force was made up mainly of the Indian XV Corps. They were assisted in their endeavour by the 81st Division – and Kakra was directly involved in the campaign.

In the process, Empire forces encountered unexpectedly fierce resistance from the Japanese.

A battalion made up mostly of Gambian soldiers suffered heavy casualties in the process.

As far as Kakra was concerned, apart from cuts and lacerations he sustained from thorns and other sharp-edged plants he came in contact with as he on some occasions was forced to crawl under the thick undergrowth, he survived the conflict almost unscathed, at least physically.

In the end, Empire forces were compelled to retreat a distance away from the Kaladan Valley and into the relative safety of the valley of another river flowing in the area, namely the Kalapanzin river.

* Third Arakan campaign

Commonwealth soldiers would not be deterred by the setback of the second Arakan campaign. After a brief spell used for training, strategy refining, etc., a force made up, as in the previous instance, of the Indian XV Corps and the 81st Division, launched another offensive in August 1944.

Re-entering the Kaladan Valley, they pounced heavily on the Japanese, forcing them to withdraw from their previously long-held positions, further afield, to a position a few miles away from the India–Burma border.

They would not be given the respite they might have wished for! Instead, they were attacked by the 82nd West African Division, which had in the meantime arrived in the conflict zone from West Africa.

Both divisions pushed the Japanese hard over the hilly, forested and sodden terrain, driving them southwards, with the goal of forcing them completely out of the Arakan. At that stage, Kakra and his brave warriors could sense victory on the horizon. The war was far from over, however – they still needed to free Myohaung, the ancient Arkanese town at the mouth of the Kaladan river from Japanese occupation. Moving from different directions, the 81st and 82nd Divisions made a push towards Myohaung, with the enemy caught in a pincer movement in between.

Chapter 40
A last-minute deflection that spared a bone

~~~

It was during this assault on Myohaung, indeed in the heat of the fierce battles in and around Myohaung, that Kakra, for the first time in his military career had his first close encounter with death.

Throughout the remainder of his life, whenever he had occasion to narrate his wartime experiences, it was this account of his own harrowing encounter with death that always brought him to tears.

It was January 19, 1945. With the 82nd Division and other units of the Empire Army, the 81st Division was engaged in a ferocious battle with the Japanese at Myohaung near the mouth of the Kaladan River. In the event, a small unit, of which he was a member, came under attack by the enemy soldiers who had taken cover behind some rocks. It was then that Kakra witnessed two of his comrades fall before his very eyes.

"Take cover, quick men!" their commanding officer ordered them.

Kakra instantly threw himself flat on the ground and began to crawl on his stomach, his heavy supply packet on his back. Initially, he thought he had escaped the unexpected assault unharmed, but he soon began to feel excruciating pain in his left thigh just above his knee. Meanwhile around him a hail of bullets kept whistling past. As he crawled along the rugged and rocky terrain past several fallen comrades, some lying in pools of blood, some with mouths agape and lifeless eyes staring sightlessly into the heavens, Kakra thought his end had come – indeed, that one or more of the bullets would at any moment hit him in the head and burn a path through his brain and, in the process, send him to an untimely death. Would anyone manage to retrieve his body, he wondered, or would he be left to the elements and his mortal remains provide a welcome dinner for one or more of the hungry Burmese wild tigers?

After creeping on all fours over a considerable distance, the sound of gunshot gradually died down. Not only did he feel exhausted and drained, the pain from the gunshot was excruciating, to put it mildly. Unable to walk both as a result of the crippling pain from his wound and also as a result of exhaustion, he only managed to crawl and hide behind a thicket, to prevent the enemy soldiers who passed by from identifying him straight away. He feared terribly for his life; indeed, he thought his end would come at any moment, that any moment could be his last.

After lying in that position for several hours, he became unconscious.

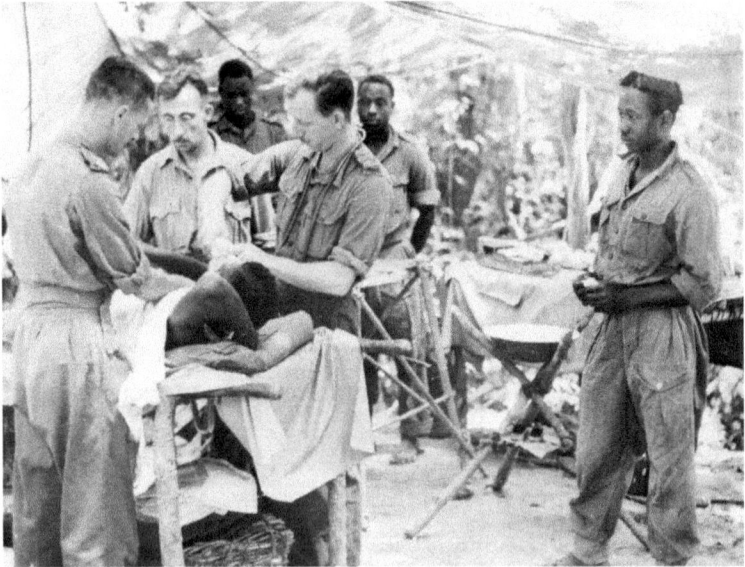

An injured West African soldier receiving treatment at a field Hospital;
Kakra underwent treatment in the same facility.
(Source: Imperial War Museum K7403)

He awoke in a field hospital. As he later learnt, the reinforcement back-up troops that his commander had requested had eventually arrived and had managed to defeat the attacking Japanese unit. They then went about retrieving the dead and the injured. At the time he was discovered, they initially took him for dead. It was after they had shouted in his ears trying to arouse him that they noticed some movement. He was quickly evacuated and sent to the field hospital where he was rushed to an improvised theatre, where the doctors battled to save his life. They managed eventually to repair a damaged blood vessel that was causing considerable blood loss, leading in the end to the stabilisation of his condition.

Had the bullet that injured him been possibly deflected prior to impact, leading it to lose velocity at the time it hit him? In any case, instead of shattering or breaking his thigh bone, it was stopped, resulting in soft tissue injury rather than a bone fracture.

This incident ended his direct involvement in the conflict. Whilst being thankful for his survival, the battle-proven warrior was somehow disappointed about the lost opportunity to witness with his own eyes the decisive hours of the battle of Myohaung.

After spending four weeks in hospital, Kakra was discharged to his jungle military camp.

As he later learnt from his mates who survived the conflict – sadly not a few of his companions had to pay the capital price – the incessant shelling of Japanese positions by the highly motivated and determined West African soldiers led the Japanese occupants to flee the town. On January 24, 1945 the town was formally declared liberated.

After the fall of Myohaung, operations of the 14th Army continued relentlessly southwards. Eventually, the Japanese were forced to evacuate the neighbouring Mayu peninsula, which they had occupied for almost four years.

As far as the brave West African soldiers were concerned, the war was then virtually over.

Concerning the Japanese occupation of Burma as a whole, it formally came to an end in May 1945.

As Kakra learnt later on, a little over two and half years after the end of the Japanese occupation, on January 4, 1948 Burma gained independence from British colonial rule. An account of the circumstances that led to their achievement of independence is, however, beyond the scope of this narration.

Chapter 41
Joy nipped in the bud

~mm~

WITH THE JOB DONE, the withdrawal of the West African troops from Burma began in March 1945.

Kakra, who, as already mentioned, was discharged back to the jungle camp after four weeks' treatment in the field medical centre, began once again to dream of the imminent reunion with Panin and the rest of his family.

On the evening of April 21, 1945, the men in Kakra's Division were ordered to get ready for their departure for India the next day. True to the directive, several vehicles turned up the next day to pick up the troops. After spending a few hours packing their belongings into the vehicles, the convoy of military trucks was set in motion, heading away from the war-torn country. Kakra and his mates were putting almost 15 months of their role in the Burma Campaign of the Second World War behind them.

Their commanders were tight-lipped as to their ultimate destination. They were only told they were heading for a transit camp in central India. Kakra assumed they were being taken to an accommodation facility nearest their port of departure to await the next available troopship to take them back home.

He would soon be disappointed. Instead of being sent to the vicinity of the nearest port to await a quick repatriation home, they were sent to a makeshift camp near the town of Kaverti Nagar, about 100 miles north-west of the port city of Madras.

Kakra thought that with his departure from Burma, he had put behind him the isolated jungle existence of South East Asia. He would soon be disillusioned about his expectations, for the location of the camp was just as lonely as, if not lonelier than, the jungle base they had just left behind.

The camp indeed was situated in a godforsaken, obscure and forlorn spot in a barren, blazing hot and dusty stretch of open country. Apart from a railway track which lay several hundred metres away, and a small railway station associated with it where hardly any train pulled to a stop during the day, the camp was almost completely cut off from the outside world.

If there was anything that spoke more favourably for this desolate camp compared to the jungle camps of Burma, it was on account of its peaceful setting; indeed, there was much comfort in the realisation that, contrary to the situation in Burma, here one could at least go to bed without having to worry about possible ambushes by the enemy!

Several weeks after their arrival, the troops were still in the dark regarding the plans made for their repatriation to their various home countries.

Chapter 42
An Englishman yearning for Africa's emancipation from the shackles of colonialism

~~~

As they waited for the opportunity to return home, resentment built up among the African soldiers, especially when it became known that the available ships were been reserved for the whites; indeed, that priority had been given to the transportation of the British.

One day after breakfast, a group of blacks spontaneously gathered in an open space not far from the main entrance to the facility. Soon the conversation turned to the matter that was fuelling considerable resentment among the group – namely the delay in transporting them back to their respective homes.

"I feel homesick, I want to go home", one of the men began.

"I am also tired of waiting! I also want to be back home."

"When are the ships coming to take us home?"

"Well, I don't know."

"I am told one is on the way."

"Reserved for the British!"

"That is disgusting, really disgusting."

"Their excuse is that their troops need to get home without delay to help in the reconstruction efforts after the destruction brought about by the war."

"What about us? We also need to carry out reconstruction in our countries."

"They are saying that the war did not directly affect our countries – that no rebuilding of destroyed buildings or homes need to be undertaken."

"I don't buy that argument; our societies are underdeveloped. We need to get home as soon as possible to help rebuild our societies, making use of the experience and skills we have acquired."

Just about that time Jack Brown, a British soldier from Leeds who had earned the nickname of Jack the African, both among the West African and also his British comrades, for his predisposition towards the African soldiers, was seen entering the facility.

Though not based in their quarter, but rather in one adjacent to the one housing mainly the West Africans, he had made it a habit to turn up on a daily basis to associate with them; it was his own little way of helping to "boost their morale", as he was wont to say.

"Jack, you realise how unfairly your people are treating us!" one of the soldiers complained as he drew nearer to them.

"Well, I really pity you", he said in a voice betraying his genuine sympathy.

"When are the ships coming to take us home?" one of the men inquired.

"If only I could tell you!" Jack replied.

"Well, we accept that the Empire is facing logistical challenges, having to take the hundreds of thousands from all continents who took part in the war back home. I would however have expected that for the sake of fairness, we would be equally treated."

"Yes, they could have arranged matters in such a way that the moment one ship leaves with troops for England, the next heads for Africa!"

"I would even be satisfied with a two-to-one cycle – two for the British masters, the next for the African slaves!"

"Don't call yourselves slaves, friend. You are free men", Jack advised.

"But we are *not* free; we live in colonies ruled by our masters – the British."

"I have on several occasions urged you to agitate for the independence of your respective countries on your return", Jack said. "Britain is almost broke, having been forced into this colossal conflict. So it won't in the next several years be financially and materially capable of facing up to any agitation for independence arising from the colonies.

"Yet another point that favours you is the psychological impact that the war certainly has had on you. Without the war, you wouldn't have had the opportunity to interact with Englishmen, the likes of Jack Brown..." he grinned.

"Jack the African!" someone interrupted him. "I am giving you that name in recognition of your concern for Africa, which I am convinced beyond doubt is genuine."

"Well, I accept the title with great honour", he smiled. "I will let my parents know when I get back to England."

Jack went on: "Yes, the war has offered you the opportunity to interact with soldiers the like of Jack the African! Now you know our weaknesses and shortcomings. You have by now surely come to realise that we are not supermen but real men – men of flesh and blood like yourselves.

"You have seen us injured, taken captive, indeed, shot and killed, just like anyone else. So why should you allow us to dictate matters to you? Well, I cannot fight your fight for you; it is up to you to grasp the golden opportunity to demand your right to govern yourselves."

"Surely, we shall carry the fight to the British!" one of the soldiers assured him.

"It is my hope that ten years from now, several, if not more, African countries will have attained independence", Jack continued. "Whichever country is the first to attain independence, one thing is certain, if I happen to be alive I will make sure I attend the celebration, never mind if I have to sell all my property to finance the trip.

Chapter 43
Panin's rollercoaster experience

—*wm*—

A T THE SAME TIME that Kakra and his mates were yearning to return home to their loved ones, their relations on their part were going through what can aptly be described as an emotional rollercoaster ride – one moment they would be up in the air, excited at the prospect of an imminent reunion, the next moment they would be plunged into despair, saddened by the prospect of having to reckon with the worst.

The situation was particularly unbearable for Panin. So long as the war raged on he had come to terms with the uncertainty surrounding the whereabouts of his soulmate. The flame of hope that he was still alive, while growing dim over the years, still kept burning in his heart. With the war over and there being seemingly no sign of Kakra returning, the uncertain situation took a terrible toll on his health and well-being.

The inhabitants of Kakra's hometown would have been kept in the dark in any case concerning the end of the war; they would be unaware of a favourable turn of events on the war front since they had no access to radio broadcasts. Indeed, at the time of Kakra's abduction up till almost five and half years thereafter, the residents of Kojokrom were virtually cut off from the outside world in the area of modern communication. None of them possessed a radio set. Indeed, one might ask, were any of them even aware of the concept of radio broadcasts?

Concerning print media, though it was gradually making headway in the Gold Coast, the few newspapers in circulation in the colony were available mainly in the major towns such as Accra, Kumasi, Cape Coast, etc.

Readers will recall the hint given to Duku and Panin by the police officer concerning the possible whereabouts of Kakra. Panin and the family at large would have liked to follow the course of the war, if only for the sake of their beloved Kakra. Unfortunately, as a result of the factors outlined above, that was hardly possible.

It was only when, once in a blue moon, residents travelled to places like Kumasi or Accra that some came back with reports about the war. Whether their accounts corresponded to the truth or were pure fabrications from their respective fantasy banks, no one could say.

The situation, as far as access to radio broadcasts was concerned, changed in the middle of 1944, thanks to the bold decision of Papiito, one of the sons of the little village, to move from Accra where he resided back to his place of birth, where he settled.

Papiito, bless him! His parents, who had in the meantime passed away, were among the few in the village who had managed to send their children to school. In the end, he acquired the Middle School leaving certificate. In his quest for a better life, he had ventured to Accra, making use of the very last of his money to pay for his transportation. After initial difficulties, he managed to find a job as a houseboy at the home of an English couple in Accra.

After being in that position for a little over four years, tragedy struck the family he was serving. One day his master developed a high temperature and was rushed to a clinic where, after a while, he sadly succumbed to his ailment.

"Malaria!" his mistress told him, hardly able to control her tears.

Having lost her husband, the lady of the home decided to return to her native England with their two little children. If she had had her own way, she would have taken Papiito with her, for he had endeared himself to her. Unable to take him with her due to bureaucratic hurdles, she decided instead to bestow on him a sum of money.

"Take good care of it, Papiito", she urged him. "I don't want you to suffer like the average person I meet daily on the streets of Accra on my way to work."

Papiito initially battled with himself as to what to do with the gift of money. After careful thought he decided in the end to return to his birthplace to engage in cocoa farming. Among the items he took along to his place of birth were a radio receiver and other belongings to restart life in the village.

He acquired a large piece of land and, with the help of hired labourers, he put his plans to go into cocoa farming into action. He also set up a shop, the first of its kind in the community.

With the arrival of a radio receiver, the dwellers were no longer completely cut off from the outside world.

Papiito's transistor radio thus became a source, not only of information, but entertainment for the little settlement. Residents frequented his shop, not only to purchase goods, but also to hang around to listen to music and to hear the news, indeed to hear the latest on the war being fought in Europe and elsewhere.

As they hung around, they would engage in lively and sometimes heated debates on various issues. Mainly as a result of the circumstances surrounding the disappearance of their two fellow citizens – most were convinced they had ended up on the battlefield – the issue of the Second World War featured prominently in their discussions.

"The English couple I served in Accra showed me a book written by Hitler titled *Mein Kampf.* In it he is said to have spoken very derogatively about black people", Papiito told those gathered around his radio listening to the news bulletin one day.

"Speaking derogatively! That is nothing", someone countered. "I have been told he has plans to burn all black people alive if he has his own way!"

"Well, I have also heard he has plans to enslave all Africans!" another alleged. "As his slaves, we would first be forced to labour on farms and factories without pay. When after a while we grow old and are no longer capable of performing the tedious duty expected of us, he would just feed us to the wild beasts."

"I would prefer to be burnt alive rather than be fed to wild animals!" someone in the group cried out. "The Black man! Why does everyone seem to look down on us? It's not our fault we are born with our skin colour. Is it?"

"They look down on us, but when it comes to fighting their wars, they forcibly recruit our sons into their armies!" another joined in.

"You are right! Just consider what has happened to Kakra and Nyamekye. They have been forcefully taken away against their will!"

"I pray every day for their safe return", another said and proceeded to voice his opinion. "Based on what I have just heard from some of you concerning the devious plans of the Germans towards the blacks, we can think of the two as doing service to the black race. What I do not find proper is the manner of their recruitment. They should have come over here, seen the chief and asked him to gather all able-bodied men for a meeting to explain the necessity for us to take up arms and confront Hitler. I personally would have voluntarily offered myself for recruitment without much hesitation! I have just heard about Hitler's intention to enslave us and eventually feed us to the beasts. Well, if I am going to die all the same, then I will not do so without resistance! If Hitler wants to kill me, then I'll fight him to the death!"

Thanks to Papiito's radio service, residents of Kojokrom got word of the unconditional surrender of Nazi Germany to Allied Forces on May 8, 1945. The news was met with wild jubilations in the settlement.

With the end of the war, Panin and the others prayed and hoped for an imminent reunion with their beloved Kakra.

After several months elapsed without any sign of the return of Kakra and his friend Nyamekye, serious doubts arose not only in the minds of the families of the two missing boys, but in the minds of the little community at large as to whether the boys had indeed been forcefully recruited into the army and sent to fight for the Empire. Were they perhaps not victims of ritual murderers who had pounced on them at an opportune time? Had they perhaps been mercilessly murdered and subsequently harvested for body parts required for the devilish ceremonies of the abductors, and then their remaining mortal parts disposed of?

Chapter 44
Mulling over an African's political future in a far distant land

~~~

AS A WAY OF keeping themselves occupied as they waited for the opportunity to embark on the journey home, the troops occupied themselves with various activities – English language classes, dramatic displays, talks, debates, sporting activities, etc.

Kakra took part in a debate on the topic: *Africa Ready for Independence, Yes or No?*

He was to speak in favour of the idea, whereas Kayode, a soldier from Nigeria, was to speak against it.

The event took the form of exchanges rather than a debate in the classical sense. A summary of the proceeding is provided below:

"In my opinion Africans, in general, are not ready for independence!" Kayode began.

"Of course we are!" Kakra countered.

"No, we are not!"

"Why not?"

"There are several reasons!"

"Go ahead and present them, I'm listening!"

"Do you really want to know?"

"Of course, I want to hear your opinion."

"Now you are talking of replacing the colonial administration with elected representatives of the indigenous population, is that right?"

"Exactly."

"You call that democracy, right?"

"Indeed; a government of the people, by the people, for the people."

"Well, by virtue of our war experience and some of the lectures we have received in the area of politics, economics, nation building, etc., we have become quite enlightened in those and other spheres of life. Now when you get back to your village, go and stand in the middle of the community and put the question 'What is democracy?' to those who pass by you – and wait and see their reaction!"

"Of course, I do not expect them to be in a position to provide a dictionary definition of the concept of democracy. One thing they can do, however – they will be in a position to vote for the person or party of their preference when called upon to do so." Kakra countered.

"On what basis? On the basis of the programme of the candidate's party, or on the basis of the tribe the party is associated with?" Kayode asked.

"It should be on the basis of the party's programme."

"But do you really think that is what is going to happen? I need not educate you on the fact that various countries on the continent of Africa, are made up of several tribes, each endowed with completely different languages.

"I cannot speak for the Gold Coast, but in Nigeria we have, to name only a few: Hausa, Igbo and Yoruba – languages differing completely from each other.

"As in the case of Nigeria, the common binding language that makes possible communication between the various tribes is the language of the respective colonial masters: English in the case of the four West African countries making up the RWAFF; French for Togo and Dahomey as examples of French colonies; Portuguese for Angola and Mozambique, etc.

"Even then, the facilitation of communication between individuals of the various tribes within a colony provided by the language of the colonial master is generally limited to the few educated members of the respective colony.

"As a result of the aforesaid, should such colonies be granted independence, politics will descend into what I will describe as 'tribal marketing', a situation in which candidates will seek to exploit their association with a particular tribe to their advantage.

"Apart from the language barrier, there are still other impediments to consider. You will agree with me that prior to the arrival of the Europeans to our shores, there were no countries as we have them today on the African map. Such countries were arbitrarily created by the colonial masters."

"I am aware of that."

"You concur with me then that the territory of the Gold Coast, for example, is an artificial creation of the Europeans?"

"Yes, I do."

"You also acknowledge the fact that prior to the arrival of the white man to our shores there were no borders, right?"

"That's correct."

"Instead there were merely tribes living in territories, without any marked boundaries?"

"Sure."

"Thanks; please allow me to continue with my argument...

"So far there has been a semblance of peace, a kind of peaceful co-existence of the various tribes. I attribute this to what I term the 'refereeing' role being played by the colonial power. What do you think will happen if there is a hasty transfer of power from the colonial administration to an indigenous one?

"We should also agree on the form of government to adopt after independence. As I stated earlier on, the various countries are made up of several tribes. Prior to the artificial creation of such countries, each tribe was being ruled by its traditional leader.

"Now, how is that going to function in the newly independent African countries?

"Will the government be formed by means of proportional representation of the various tribes, or will it be based on which party wins the most votes cast?

"We should guard against a situation whereby the smaller tribe or tribes of a particular independent country would feel marginalised by the majority ethnic group. These are fundamental issues that need to be addressed prior to becoming independent."

Kayode paused for a while to have a sip of water from a cup beside him. The assembled listeners, judging from their facial expressions, appeared to be enjoying the exchanges; they remained quiet and attentive.

"Please allow me to continue my case.

"I must say, some observations that I have made about our people are very worrying to me, a fact that has led me to become very sceptical about the prospect of self-rule."

"What do you mean by that?"

"I am indeed bothered about the tendency of many of us – I don't think I am completely innocent in that regard – to think only about our selfish interests rather than the common good of all!"

"Well, that is a human trait that is not peculiar to Africans alone, surely?"

"Are you sure that is a universal shortcoming?"

"To err is human; no one is perfect!"

"Still, I think that trait is too pervasive with our people. We seem to think about our self alone, rather than the common interest. I won't be surprised to find a situation when, after we have gained self-rule, the funds earmarked for state projects will end up in the pockets of certain individuals rather than be used for the purpose for which it was intended!"

"Of course, I do not dispute that. There will however be checks and balances in the system to prevent something like that happening."

"Are you sure the checks and balances will work?"

"We are duty-bound to ensure they do."

"Well, I remain sceptical."

"I am optimist by nature."

"Well, your optimism should not lead you to close your eyes to the hard realities."

"I have taken that into account. Are you resting you case?

"Not done yet!"

At that moment, he cast a glance at the audience and pleaded: "Please, please bear with me a little longer." After a moment's silence he said, "Thanks; I will continue.

"I want to turn my attention to one issue, namely the issue of our extended family system and the problems that it could pose in the period of self-rule. Let us assume I am given a position as a minster! All of a sudden, all family members, brothers, sisters, nieces, nephews, yes, everyone who shares even a very distant relationship or association with me, would want to derive some favour from me. Woe unto me if I am unable to meet their various needs! That inevitably will lead to nepotism, tribalism, favouritism, etc."

"I fully understand your fears. To mitigate that, we need to introduce the concept of the welfare state."

"What do you mean by that?"

"In a welfare state, the state sees it as a responsibility to cater for the needs of every citizen. Thus, instead of turning to a member of the external family for help in time of need, that individual will apply to the government for assistance."

"That sounds very interesting indeed. But do you think it will work in our situation? Won't the individual entrusted with the money keep everything for him or herself instead of passing it on to the intended beneficiary or beneficiaries?"

"We will have to rely on the checks and balances to be built into the system!"

"Gentlemen, I am afraid I do not share the optimism of my fellow speaker. The checks and balances he is proposing just won't work! I still hold the opinion we are just not ready for self-rule. We are surely going to mess things up when given the opportunity to rule ourselves without adequate preparations."

"So, when do you think we shall be ready?"

"Well, I don't want to set any time-frame. First and foremost we need to educate the populace and develop a political culture, a culture that will lead us to think and vote on important issues and not according to tribal lines."

"I agree with you on the need to educate the population. But that will not happen so long as we are under colonial rule. Friend, do you think it is in the interest of the colonial masters to educate us?

"Take my case as an example. I would surely have loved to go to school. But our parents could not afford it. It is a strategy of the colonialist – to keep the populace uneducated and, in so doing, make it easy to rule over them. Of course, they are not unaware of the dangers posed to their authority by a highly enlightened populace!

"One way they seek to achieve their goal is to limit the creation of new schools as much as possible and use high fees as a way of preventing as many children as possible from taking advantage of the few available schools."

"You may be right in your assertion; still, it is my conviction that we need to approach the matter of independence cautiously and gradually; a time will surely come in the future when we will be ripe enough to rule ourselves."

"Our independence certainly will not come in our lifetime if we were to adopt your approach!" Kakra countered. "Take it from me, the colonial masters will only voluntarily depart from our land – if ever they will – after they have completely plundered everything they can lay hands on here – gold, diamonds, bauxite, timber, etc. Indeed, if we fail to apply some kind of pressure to force them out, they will stay on indefinitely.

"As you are aware, we have interacted with several British as well as quite a good number of Polish soldiers on the battlefield.

"I like them as human beings. They displayed strengths and weaknesses, just like any other human being. We saw them scared, injured, suffering, indeed, dying, just like anyone else.

"So I now ask myself: why should I be subjected to the likes of our comrades – like Jack Brown a.k.a. Jack the African, Robert May, Peter Corbyn, Gordon Blaire, Nigel Farron – you can go on naming them?! Is it because of their light skin colour?

"Prior to the arrival of the Europeans on our shores, we managed our affairs alright. Why do we need them to instruct us on how to go about our daily life?"

"Well, whether we like it or not, by dint of history, they have become our colonial masters. The question now is – how do we disentangle ourselves from them? I want to make one thing clear. I am also in favour of African independence. We differ only on the approach, in particular on the speed. Whereas you are calling for a speedy transition, I am calling for a gradual approach."

"If we go by your method, it will take us ages to attain our independence!"

"Better to go slowly and land safely, than to rush and crash-land!"

"We should rather go with the momentum of the present time, indeed take advantage of the momentum created by the events of this war. Postponing matters into the unforeseeable future, in my opinion, is not prudent."

"Mr Chairman, I do hereby rest my case!"

"Your closing words, please", the Chairman turned to Kakra's opponent.

"Well, I am still not convinced by the arguments of my fellow comrade in arms.

"As I touched upon earlier on, in my opinion our people need more time to prepare for independence.

We have to educate them on the concept of statehood, of democracy, of the rights and obligations of citizens in a state, etc. It is only after we have built a reasonably good foundation that, in my opinion, we should seek self-rule."

"Any time frame?" the Chairman wanted to know.

"I don't want to throw any figures into the air; time will tell."

"Thank you very much for the lively exchange. I hereby declare the meeting closed."

Amidst a rousing applause, the meeting dispersed.

Kakra was pleased he had, at least on the day in question, helped kill some time for himself and his compatriots tormented by the scourge of chronic boredom.

Chapter 45

West African fury over non-recognition of precious lives lost

―――

TO WHILE AWAY THE TIME, one day Kakra and his mates gathered for a game of cards. As in several other meetings in the past, the conversation soon turned to the matter of the delay in sending them home.

"Why have they moved us from one secluded location to another? I really thought they were sending us home!"

"And the communication is bad; no one is telling us anything!"

"We have had to endure one form of discrimination after the other; and now this! Couldn't they have corralled us into a camp in a friendlier location? I did not expect them to book us into a posh hotel in the middle of Bombay, naturally. Still, they could surely have provided us with accommodation in a more congenial, ambient place with better access to the outside world!"

"Is this the first time you are sensing discrimination, my friend? Let us take the issue of our pay structure – you are aware that a British soldier with the basic rank of private is paid more than a non-commissioned officer from West Africa, aren't you?"

"Say it again, my brother!"

"That is outrageous, really outrageous!" another joined in.

"Let us move to the area of commissioned officers. Apart from Captain Seth Anthony, the officer from the Gold Coast we spoke of recently, there is no African officer... only European and Indian officers."

"My unit commander was English."

"Mine was Polish. Initially I took him to be English, until he introduced himself and revealed he was Polish."

"The Polish! There were quite a good deal of them. How did they come to be in the Army in the first place?"

"Well, my understanding is that they fled to Britain after their country had been overrun by the Germans. As a way of helping to defeat the Nazis, they volunteered to fight on the side of the British. My understanding is there are between 300 and 400 in the 14th Army.

"I don't have anything against them; my unit commander, for example, was a brilliant commander. The point I am making is that had they given us Africans the opportunity, we too could have excelled, in just the same way as our *brother*, Capt Seth Anthony has done."

"They may argue that there are not enough blacks sufficiently qualified for the position!"

"'Seek and you will find', as the saying goes! If they had sought they would have found qualified men – I might even say *well-qualified* candidates roaming the streets of places like Ibadan, Lagos, Accra, Kumasi, Freetown, Banjul, etc."

"You are right! It is part of the strategy of the army leadership to exclude blacks from the top military hierarchy!"

"So, they need us only for the dirty work?"

"Of course! Do you think they brought us all the way from Africa to make us commissioned officers? No; just to fight and eventually get killed. And if we die – who cares?"

"A few black men less in the world population!"

"Good news for those who consider us to be good for nothing!"

"Just occupying space, and breathing oxygen for nothing!"

"What have we done wrong, friends?"

"You should best put that question to your Creator, if you believe there is a Creator – if not, then so be it."

A short silence followed, broken a moment later by Solaga, a recruit from the Trans-Volta territory of the Gold Coast. According to him, he had signed up for the army at the age of just 17, "in search of adventure" – as he put it.

"Men", he said, "I have been following your conversation. Initially I did not want to join in the discussion, since I have repeatedly expressed

169

my anger and disgust about our current situation without anyone taking the slightest bit of notice! So, I have just resigned myself to my fate. What I heard from one of our Indian mates I spoke to when I went out jogging in the morning has led me to become even more angry and frustrated."

"What did he tell you?" Kakra wanted to know.

"I don't want to tell you – in order not to break your hearts!"

"In that case you should not have mentioned it to us! Now you have aroused my curiosity!"

"Friend, you better let the cat out of the bag!" another insisted. "After all we have endured so far, I don't think anything could be worse than what we have already endured."

"Okay, then, here goes. You are surely aware Burma is not the only Empire territory that has been invaded by the Japanese. Just by way of a reminder – even prior to their invasion of Burma, they had occupied Honk Kong, Singapore, the Malay Islands, etc. Now according to my Indian acquaintance, who claims to have good contacts with higher places within the army, plans are well-advanced to send us to reclaim the Malay Islands from the Japanese!"

"Stop it!"

"No more of that!!"

"I'd rather point my own gun at myself, at my skull and blow my brain out than allow myself to be commandeered into yet another battlefield!"

"Well, I cannot say with 100 per cent certainty that what he told me is true. I consider him credible though; whatever he has revealed to me in the past has turned out to be true."

"Damn, shit!"

"Well, according to my source, they are so impressed with what we have accomplished, that they are confident we will be able to quickly end the Japanese occupation of the said islands."

"That is outrageous!" Kakra burst out. "If they are so impressed with what we have achieved, why did General William Slim, the GOC commanding the 14th Army, fail even to mention our name in his victory speech! Yes, he thanked the British, the Indians, the Gurkhas, the Poles, etc., for their contribution – but not the West Africans!! Now they want to deploy the 'silly' West Africans in yet another battlefield!"

"You are indeed right! He just chose to ignore us!"

"Come to think about it – we achieved an amazing feat in an almost impossible setting, yet the GOC did not consider it worth mentioning!" Kakra lamented.

"Heartbreaking, really heartbreaking! So our brothers who shed their blood in the conflict – in the 81st and 82nd Divisions that lost a little over 2,500 men – have died in vain!" Solaga stated.

"The GOC does not thank us? You know me, my English no good, so I no follow everything he say. I just clap, clap, clap!" said Akinbode, a Nigeria comrade who told them his name stood for "a warrior has arrived".

"Clap, clap, clap, when you no understand! Eh? My friend from Oyo, in Nigeria!" Kakra remarked.

"Yes, me, I, thought he was thanking everybody!"

"Well, now you understand!"

"Very bad; bad, bad!"

"Yes indeed", Kojo Essien, an otherwise reserved fellow from Takoradi, joined in the conversation. "Thank God I survived, so I don't care if he doesn't appreciate my effort. But for the sake of our fallen comrades, yes to honour our fearless, lionhearted and indomitable comrades who paid the capital price in fighting for King and Empire, whose mortal remains cannot be repatriated back to their loved ones but must rest in unmarked graves by jungle tracks, in isolated graves or cemeteries in Burma and India or in larger cemeteries in Burma the likes of Dalet Chaung near Tamandu and the Taukyan War Cemetery, the GOC could have added just a line: 'Thank you men from the 81st and 82nd for your sacrifice!' But no, he just chose to ignore us!"

"And now if what Solaga is saying is true, they are contemplating deploying us in other conflict zones!"

"If they don't respect us, then they should leave us in peace now to return home to our loved ones instead of sending us to yet another battlefield!"

"Of course! I also yearn to return home to see my family as soon as possible. Unfortunately, there is little we can do; we are subject to the whims and caprices of our colonial masters. You are in their army; whether by choice or by coercion is irrelevant. You are a soldier, and soldiers have to obey the orders of their superiors. Besides that, you are about 10,000 kilometres from home. How are you going to get there on your own?"

Over the next several days, the gossip, instead of ceasing, continued to spread, to the extent that almost everyone reckoned with an imminent directive from the leadership to get ready for the Malay undertaking.

Chapter 46
Mankind's self-annihilation weapons in action

―*ₘₘ*―

W HILE KAKRA and the other Gold Coast troops were coming to terms with the prospect of being sent to the battlefields of Malay to help fight the occupying Japanese forces there, he joined other mates for a game of football on a makeshift pitch they had recently constructed on their own.

On his return to the base after kicking the ball around for about an hour, he noticed an unusually large number of the troops had gathered around the TV in the common room. Out of curiosity he popped in to find out what it was that had drawn the crowd.

"Terrible, terrible!" one of the soldiers told him just as he entered the hall.

"What is the matter?"

"A massive, massive bomb has been dropped on the Japanese!"

"Really? By whom?"

"By the Amis. According to the report, it was dropped on Hiroshima at around 9:15 a.m. local time. Yes indeed. Just this morning, local time, the Amis dropped a huge bomb on the city of Hiroshima. Words cannot describe the destruction caused by the monstrous bomb. You just draw close and see things for yourself."

Kakra did as advised. He was so appalled at what he saw that he decided to quit the room just as quickly as he had got there.

The destruction brought about by the bomb was heinous, just beyond comprehension.

Even though he had just been exposed to the news momentarily, what he saw would haunt him for several days, if not weeks thereafter.

Throughout the night he pondered on the matter. If mankind would not learn to settle misunderstandings by way of peaceful negotiations rather than by force, it would surely just be a matter of time before they would, through their own making, bring about the annihilation of all forms of life on the planet! Or so he surmised.

Two days later the TV newsreel carried reports of the dropping of yet another bomb on a Japanese city, this time on Nagasaki.

"How long will it be before the powers that be in Japan feel the need to surrender?" Kakra wondered. "Will they wait until their capital Tokyo is also wiped out before doing so?"

Then finally, on August 15, 1945, news of the surrender of the Japanese to the Allies a day before broke out in the camp.

Kakra joined other troops of the 81st in spontaneous outbursts of joy. More than ever, the likelihood of an imminent return home had become tangible, he reasoned. Throughout the rest of the day, the whole community was in a state of euphoria. Before long someone went around gathering contributions together with the goal of acquiring a bull for a big feast. Soon the sum needed for the acquisition was attained. A delegation was dispatched without delay to the nearest available cattle market to purchase the bull.

It was too late to prepare the feast that evening, so matters were postponed to the following day. In the evening, the whole community gathered in a large open space for the feast! With the prospect of a possible operation in the Malay Islands now out of the question following the events of the previous day, everyone, including Kakra, looked forward to a speedy repatriation back home.

However, those who had hoped for a speedy return home following the surrender of the Japanese would soon be disappointed. Several, weeks after the capitulation of the Japanese, there was still no word or sign of an imminent departure.

What fomented the indignation of the troops further was their realisation that somehow, their British officers had managed, as it were, to sneak away and head back home, leaving their troops behind – just in the way a captain of a stricken ship might have taken a lifeboat to safety and left his awe-stricken passengers behind to sort out things on their own!

Chapter 47
A missed opportunity

~~~

O NE DAY as Kakra was heading for the canteen to have a meal, he heard loud cries coming from the wing of the barracks housing mainly troops from Sierra Leone.

The shouts and cries grew louder and louder.

Out of curiosity, he decided to draw near to ascertain what the matter was.

Soon he caught up with some of the men who had poured out of their rooms to observe matters from the large open yard overlooking the nearby building that housed the Sierra Leonean troops.

"What the hell is going on there?" he inquired from one of them.

"A fight; a real fist fight!"

"That's dreadful. Why, and who is engaged in the squabble?"

"It's between some Sierra Leonean soldiers on the one hand, and some Gambian troops on the other!"

"But why?"

"Some Sierra Leonean troops have gone on the rampage. I understand they have attacked their commander. In the process, they sought to gain access to the armoury, to get hold of weapons! The Gambian soldiers on guard there resisted the attempt, a situation that has led to a fierce exchange of blows. I hope no one comes to harm."

"That should not happen among our African brothers!"

"Well my friend, this long wait is driving people to desperation, and they are growing wild. Unless those who brought us here take immediate steps to rectify the situation, indeed, send us back home without delay, people will really go bananas!"

"You're right, man! These days, out of sheer boredom, I have increasingly developed the habit of talking to myself. I'll surely go mental if things continue like this!"

In the course of the day, further details concerning the causes of the melee between the West African soldiers emerged.

Apparently it all started when a group of Sierra Leonean soldiers seized their commander and gave him a real beating. Fortunately, he managed to escape from their hands before they could possibly beat him to death.

The mutineers then headed for the armoury in an attempt to collect weapons to shoot at anyone who came their way.

Eventually, the Gambians succeeded in beating back the looters, thus preventing what could possibly have ended up in an awful shedding of blood.

What caused the Sierra Leoneans to lose their tempers in the first place?

The reason given was so banal that Kakra wondered how it could have escalated to the point described above. It revolved around a disagreement on haircut allowances! Under normal circumstance that should not have led to a mutiny by a large number of soldiers. Fuelled by the anger that had built up as a result of their long wait for the opportunity to return home, a small spark seemed enough to set their fire ablaze.

In the end the mutineers were court-martialled; those found guilty received prison sentences.

* * *

It was not only within the ranks of the Sierra Leoneans that trouble brewed. In October 1945, several Gold Coast soldiers, disgruntled by the long wait and aggrieved by the perceived discrimination against them by the military authorities for placing them at the back of the queue in the allocation of vessels to transport them back home, went on strike and refused to obey orders.

Just before things really get out of hand, to the extent that the West Africans were on the verge of starting an insurrection, entertaining perhaps the crazy idea of marching all the way from India to the imperial capital of London to present their petition to the King of the Empire, the news made its rounds that a ship had at last become available and that the process of their repatriation was to begin.

That was surely good news. Kakra was, however, aware that it did not immediately signify his particular repatriation. Though many had lost their lives, there were still tens of thousands of recruits who needed to be repatriated.

Kakra was kept in the dark as to the criteria employed in the selection of the troops who were privileged to leave. Whether by accident or design, a good majority of those who had engaged in the protests were part of the first batch to be given the opportunity to leave on November 6, 1945.

Kakra had to wait several months after the beginning of the repatriation for his turn to embark on the journey home.

Did the sudden availability of ships following their strike embolden Kakra's countrymen who had embarked on their protest to carry out even further actions to, as it were, test the resolve of the Empire even further?

In any case, as Kakra later found out from some of his mates who were privileged to travel on that troopship, unrest broke out not long after they had boarded the ship and set sail on their homeward journey. It began when some of the soldiers began to complain about almost everything on board the ship – the food, the drinks, the sleeping arrangements.

Things came to a head when the captain of the Dutch-registered troopship *SS Ruys* had to make an unscheduled docking at Port Said, an Egyptian city at the northern end of the Suez Canal on November 11, 1945.

With the Mediterranean and the Suez Canal safe from Nazi threat, the return journey took that route instead of sailing around the Cape of Good Hope.

Shortly after the stop, up to eight well-armed British soldiers and military police officers came on board to attempt to quell the trouble. In the melee that followed one policeman was stabbed while 50 men were arrested.

Chapter 48
Twins attracted

~~~

FACED WITH BOREDOM and with no officers in sight to restrain their movement, everyone did what he wished to kill the time. Kakra made once or twice-weekly trips to the next major town which was about half an hour's rail journey from their base.

On one such visit, as he strolled through town with about half a dozen of his mates, he felt suddenly unwell. Was it due to his early breakfast, he wondered? Soon he felt nauseous. Moments later he had to excuse himself and rush to an isolated place to vomit.

On his return, the group members noticed all was not well with their friend.

Echoing the sentiments of the others, Omoshigo, a mate from Nigeria, patted him on the shoulder and began:

"Friend, I suggest you return to the barracks to have some rest."

"Yes indeed", Kakra replied. "I thought as much. I was about to inform you about just that."

"Are you able to make the journey alone or do you want one of us to accompany you?" Omoshigo inquired.

"Thanks for the offer. I think I will be fine though."

"Sure?"

"Yes indeed."

"Okay, we will see you later."

"Take good care of yourself, mate", Nii Odarmetey, who had remained Kakra's close associate since his conscription urged him. "If any Indian you come across tries to misbehave, don't allow yourself to

179

be intimidated! Let that individual know you are a battle-proven, battle-hardened soldier who has survived ferocious conflicts in the merciless and unforgiving terrain of the Burmese jungle."

Parting company with his mates, Kakra headed for the train station which was a few hundred yards away.

Just as he reached the train station, he felt the urgent need to visit the toilet. Looking around, he saw nothing that resembled a toilet. He turned to a young lady who happened to be near him and asked:

"Excuse me please; any toilet here?"

"Come along", she said, "I will show you where it is."

So saying, she led him to a building about 50 yards away from the station. As they approached it, Kakra saw the inscription "Gents" written on one of the doors.

"That's the men's toilet", she said, pointing to the door.

"Thanks so much gracious lady."

"You are welcome."

Kakra reached the toilet just in time to avoid what would have been an embarrassment. He seemed to be developing a running stomach as well. Had the cheese served at breakfast gone bad, contaminated with disease-bringing bacteria?

He thought the lady would have gone on her way, but no, she was still nearby.

"I noticed from your facial expression that you were not feeling well", she said. "I wanted just to know whether you would want me to direct you to a nearby chemist shop. It is situated in an obscure place and only locals like me who are quite familiar with the place know where to find it.

"It is very kind of you; don't worry, I think I will be alright. It began as upset stomach; now it is developing into diarrhoea as well. I only hope the train will not be delayed so I can make it back as soon as possible."

"May I know where you are heading for?"

"The military base."

"Oh I see; I think it should arrive in about 20 minutes. I am heading in a different direction; my train is expected in about 15 minutes."

They had in the meantime got to the station. Kakra took a seat. He thought the stranger would leave him alone, but she took a seat beside him. As she did so, Kakra turned to look at her, just at the same time she also turned in his direction and their eyes met. She was not only attractive; she wore a perfume with a mesmerising fragrance.

He was enjoying her company, but the fact that he was not feeling well made him less inclined to engage her in conversation. He did not want to voice his feelings openly in order not to embarrass her. He thought she would read his body language and understand. Nevertheless, she wouldn't leave him in peace.

"American or African?" she inquired.

"Why do you want to know?"

"Out of curiosity."

"Well, I am from Africa."

"Which part of Africa?"

"The Gold Coast."

"The Gold Coast?"

"Yes indeed; any idea where it is located on a map of Africa?"

"East Africa, perhaps?"

"Not exactly."

"West Africa?"

"Yes, it lies between Trans Volta Togoland in the east, Ivory Coast in the west, Upper Volta in the north and the Atlantic Ocean to the south."

"Oh, I see; my uncle, my father's elder brother, is in Uganda."

"That is East Africa!"

"Exactly. By the way, what are you doing in India?"

"I told you I am heading for the army camp, so you may guess what I have been here for."

"Are you part of the Imperial troops sent to Burma to fight the Japanese?"

"Exactly; I am part of the Royal West African Expedition Force dispatched to Burma to confront the Japanese."

"So you travelled all the distance from Africa for that purpose?"

"Yes indeed."

"I don't get it. Our neighbour, who happens to be in the army, tells us they have recruited a huge number of Indians to fight in Burma and elsewhere. I thought the Indians could do the job alone, without the need for those responsible to ferry you over several thousands of miles to join in the fight."

"Well, I am an ordinary soldier with the rank of lance corporal, not able to influence the course of events. Maybe, the decision makers wanted to create the impression it was a conflict between two empires, the Japanese Empire on the one hand and the British on the other. So, they decided to involve troops from other Imperial territories – the Gold Coast, Nigeria, Sierra Leone, Australia, etc."

"I am told the Burma jungle is very thick, so they thought perhaps that you were more fitted to fight there."

"That may well be the case."

A short silence followed.

Kakra thought his new-found friend would leave him in peace at this juncture, but no, the young lady who appeared quite chatty resumed the conversation.

"As I mentioned earlier on, one of our neighbours is in the Army – he was also sent to fight in Burma."

"Well, there were several Indians in my unit; who knows, maybe I came across him."

"Lance Corporal Patel is his name; quite tall and a well-built fellow – not a typical Indian as far as his physique goes."

"Well, I came across a few Patels in the army as a whole. I did not know each Indian in my regiment by name, but as far as I can remember there was no Patel amongst them."

A short silence was broken again by the lady beside him.

"What do you make of the British?"

"Well, well..." Kakra hesitated.

"Well, I don't like them, at least not as colonial masters. I really wish they would leave India, sooner rather than later – tomorrow if possible! That's the reason why I whole-heartedly support Gandhi!"

"Well, you interrupted me just as I was about to express my opinion. Indeed, I am also not a fan of the Empire. I would never have joined this force of my own volition – circumstances beyond my control brought me into this situation."

"So you didn't join voluntarily? What happened?"

"Well, I don't want to go into details on that matter – not on my first meeting with a strange Indian lady, even if I find her attractive and most adorable!"

"Thanks for the compliment!"

"It's not a compliment; it's a fact."

"Gentleman, you are so pleasant to talk to! This should surely not be our last meeting. Very soon my train will be arriving. What about arranging a second meeting?"

"I have nothing against it."

Just at that moment Kakra had the feeling he was about to vomit, and the young lady noticed it.

"Oh, I better stop bothering you with my incessant talking!" she smiled with a look of concern.

"I'm really enjoying the exchange. As you can gather, however, I am not feeling very well."

"We can meet next week at the same time and place if you wish. I'm a teacher at the Catholic Primary school. I come here on Mondays; stay on till Friday and travel back home – in a little town about half an hour's ride on the train.

"It suits me. We have finished our tour of duty and are awaiting ships to take us back home. A good deal of our English officers have sneaked home already. We are left on our own – with abundance of time at our disposal."

"That's great! I'll see you next week then. Unless the unexpected happens, I'll be here at any rate. Please hang around and wait in case I am late. We have limited teaching staff, so my head may ask me to deputise for someone else, which may delay my coming."

Just at that moment she spotted a train heading towards the station.

"It's my train; yours should follow in a few minutes' time."

Just as she got up to go, she turned to Kakra.

"Ach, I even forgot to ask your name!"

"Kakra; and you?"

"Sunitha."

"Okay; goodbye Sunitha; see you soon!"

"Same to you K-a-k-a... did I get it right?"

"Not quite; it is Kakra."

"Okay, Kakra; see you soon."

Not long after her train had departed, Kakra's own pulled to stop at the station.

As he sat in the train, he pondered over the meeting with the stranger.

What a startling young lady she was! Her broad forehead, her perfectly arched eyebrows, her broad black eyes, long black hair, graceful demeanour – a real epitome of feminine attractiveness and charm!

Ever since their arrival some of his mates had returned from their short excursions into town with accounts of their chance encounters with individuals of the opposite sex in various adventurous settings. They had urged him to join them on such trips. Though he had taken part in normal daytime excursions to various places, he had all along resisted the temptation to engage in what his mates termed "adventures".

This was a lady he was keen to get to know a bit more closely. In view of his limited time in India, the idea of a meaningful "adventure" seemed to him as little more than wishful thinking on his part.

After about 20 minutes' journey on the train, his condition improved, and before long the train pulled to a stop at the station serving his camp.

As he lay in bed the night prior to the arranged meeting with Sunitha, he began to have doubts as to the advisability of attending the meeting. Indeed, for a while an inner voice urged him to stay away. On second thoughts, however, he decided against the idea of abandoning the meeting, in particular in order not to disappoint her. "When you give your word, you need to honour it, especially since you have no means of letting her know you would not be attending", another voice within him told him.

Another factor that spoke in favour of the meeting was the opportunity it offered to kill time, if only for a few hours.

On the appointed day, he left the barracks early for the meeting. Concerning his departure for home, he and his fellow soldiers were still in a limbo as to the exact date.

He arrived at the train station about half an hour prior to the appointed time.

After waiting for over 45 minutes without any sign of her showing up, he began to wonder if she would turn up at all. With her words

"Do wait – I may be called upon to deputise for someone else" ringing in his mind, he decided to hang on for a while. About almost an hour after the appointed time, just when he was considering giving up and returning to the barracks, he spotted her! She approached him from the main entrance of the station, but she was not alone.

She was in the company of her sister; not an ordinary sister, but her twin sister; furthermore, not an ordinary twin sister, but an identical twin sister, one who looked bafflingly exactly like herself!

But for the fact that they had chosen to put on a dress, which though of the same make displayed different colours – yellow for Sunitha and pink for her twin sister – they were virtually indistinguishable. Even then, as they took a stance just in front of him, their gazes fixed at him, Kakra could not make out which of the two he had met the previous occasion!

At that moment, they began as if with a single voice: "Hey, brave soldier from Africa, we have a puzzle for you – which one of us is Sunitha?"

"Both of you!" Kakra replied, laughing.

"So you cannot tell us apart? Not by virtue of our voices, perhaps?"

"Well, if I were to get to know both of you over a longer period of time, I may be able to distinguish between your voices. For the moment, however, I am at a loss!"

"From our eyes, then?"

"No; just as in the case of your voice, I will need some time to be able to make the distinction. So please help me out, otherwise I will continue to refer to each of you as Sunitha."

"Okay; we do not have much time at our disposal to wait that long. So, pay attention as we introduce ourselves."

At that stage one of them stopped talking whilst the other did the introduction.

"I am Anitha. Today, you may call me the lady in pink; that is Sunitha, my senior sister, the lady you spoke with, the lady in yellow."

"Now you know the difference", Sunitha smiled. "Beware, though", she continued, "do not think that next time we meet we will be wearing the same type of dresses. Sometimes, just to confuse others, we interchange our dresses. So next time we meet, Anitha may be the woman in yellow and Sunitha in pink – on other occasions, we may be wearing blue and green respectively. Of course, there are instances when we choose just to put on a dress of the same colour!"

At that stage Kakra chose to elucidate, for he was a twin himself!

"I have heard others say that different sets of twins are inclined to be attracted to each other. Though I have so far not made much out of that belief, events of recent days have led me to believe there may be an element of truth in the matter, indeed that the saying is not completely devoid of truth.

"Indeed, I am inclined to think it was not coincidental that Sunitha was the very first person I spoke to at the train station as I looked out for a toilet. Instead, a mystical force acting on twins served to draw us together!"

On hearing that both of the girls asked as if with a single voice:

"Are you also a twin?"

"Precisely!"

"That is weird, really weird!" Anitha remarked, visibly surprised.

"A really bizarre set of circumstances!" Sunitha exclaimed. "I see an African in need, I give assistance, and it turns out that he shares a characteristic unique to a very few set of individuals on our planet!"

"Yes indeed, I have a twin brother", Kakra said. "I am the younger of the two. Indeed, my full name is Attah Kakra. Attah is the name given to a male twin in the Akan population group to which I belong – Kakra is the junior, Panin the senior. We are not only twins, but just as in your case, also identical – hardly anyone can tell us apart."

"That's incredible!" Anitha remarked.

"So where is Panin?" Sunitha inquired.

"Back home in the Gold Coast!"

"Why did you leave him alone? He will be missing you!"

"Not only is he missing me, I miss him every day of my life!"

"So why didn't he come along with you – was he afraid to join the army?"

"I did not plan to join the army; I found myself in the Force as a result of circumstances beyond my control."

"Do you have a picture of him?"

"Sorry, I do not."

"Why not?"

"Well, we grew up in a little town; no such facilities are available there!"

"Why didn't he come along? He must be missing you!"

"And what are the circumstances you mentioned?"

At that juncture, Kakra revealed the circumstances that had led him to be part of the army, explaining how he had been abducted.

"That is really disgusting!" Anitha began.

"Have you had any contact with him since then?"

"No."

"Really?"

"We live in a little town. There is no post office there; the road leading there is also bad, so there is hardly any communication between the little settlement and the outside world."

"That must be very hard for him. I can imagine how much he is suffering. You yourself are at least aware you are still alive. The situation is completely different in his case; he may well believe you are dead."

"You are indeed right!"

"Let's find somewhere to sit so we can talk a bit further."

As Kakra looked around he realised the eyes of almost everyone around was directed at them. He wondered about the kind of thoughts that were going through the minds of the inquisitive onlookers! 'How did this African man get to know these attractive twin sisters?!'

They took a seat in one corner of the station, the two sisters facing their African friend. Kakra was the first to speak.

"Sunitha and Anitha, very fascinating names!"

"Oh, you love our names? Thanks."

"Indeed, they sound lovely. Do they have any meaning?"

"They are popular Hindu names for twins."

"Oh, so you are Hindus?"

"Indeed, the majority of Indians are Hindus."

"If you wouldn't mind, I'd like to ask you a few questions about your religion."

"Well, we are not very religious; we will be able though to give you a broad outline of what our religion entails."

"Well, before I proceed, I will let you know that I am a Catholic, though not a devoted one. I am sure you have a broad idea of Christianity."

187

"Well, I am a Hindu teaching at a Catholic primary school, so I have a general knowledge of your religion. By the way, it may interest you to know that Anitha applied for an appointment in the same school. Although they were looking to employ a few teachers and Anitha was qualified, the headteacher refused to employ her – for the simple reason that the children and the staff would have problems telling us apart! Fortunately, Anitha got a job at a government primary school not very far from mine. Now go ahead with your questions."

"Well, before I put my question, I want to give you some background. On our way from West Africa to Burma, we made stops in several Indian towns and cities – Bombay, Calcutta, Chittagong, etc. We spent several days in Calcutta. Not only myself, but all my mates were surprised at the large number of beggars on the streets – some were on the point of starvation…"

"Don't you have beggars in West Africa?"

"Of course there are beggars in our society; but the numbers we saw in Calcutta were way beyond our expectations. We were touched, in particular by those on the point of starvation, and we decided one day to collect donations of canned corned beef from our food rations to present to some of those on the streets. Somehow some of our Indian mates at the barracks got to know about our plans.

"'No, no, no!' they said, 'Keep your food.'

"'Why?' we asked, surprised.

"'No one will accept it.'

"'Why not?' we asked.

"'Didn't you get a briefing on Indian culture prior to coming here?' our Indian mates asked.

"'Well, our training and subsequent dispatch into Indian culture took place in such a rush that no one found the time to provide us with that information.'

"'Well, then take it from me… Hindus do not consume beef.'

"'Why not?' I asked.

"'It is a long story; just let this answer suffice you for the time being!'

"That the Indian colleague was telling the truth has in the meantime not only been confirmed by others, but also by the number of cattle that I frequently came across roaming in the streets of India.

"Still, I am yet to find someone to offer an explanation as to why that is the case. So, dear Sunitha and Anitha, can you please provide a brief background knowledge to the Hindu religion and, secondly, explain why adherents of the religion generally abstain from eating beef.?

"Okay, we shall do our best to do as required. In return, I will also ask you at the end of our talk to provide me with some information on a matter dear to my heart – related to your country."

"What then?"

"I want to keep you in suspense for now!"

"Anitha, if you will agree with me, I will take the first question; you will take the second."

"Agreed!" Anitha replied.

"Just before you start; just a point of interest: Do you always agree on every issue?"

"What about you and Panin?" Anitha countered with a question instead of giving an answer.

"I put the question first, so you need to answer first", Kakra insisted.

"Of course, we are humans like anyone else. Though we agree on most issues, there are occasional disagreements."

"The same is true of ourselves", Kakra stated.

Instead of leaving them alone he looked at both sternly in the eye and asked:

"What do you usually quarrel over – over which of you gets preference over a young man who makes approaches to you?"

"Hey, good soldier from West Africa! Do you want to know every detail about our private life at the very first meeting?"

"Of course not!"

"Okay, then let's give Sunitha the chance to begin her lecture."

"Okay", Sunitha agreed, "Here goes:

"Hinduism is the religion of the majority of people in India. If I am right, Christians look to Christ as the founder of Christianity; Muslims on their part assign the same role to Mohammed. You have recently come out of Burma. As you certainly noticed during your stay, Buddhism, which is the religion of the Burman majority ethnic group, credits Buddha as its founder.

"On the contrary, Hinduism has no single founder, no single scripture, and no commonly agreed set of teachings.

"Throughout its history, there have been many key figures teaching different philosophies and writing numerous holy books. For these reasons, writers often refer to Hinduism as 'a way of life' or 'a family of religions' rather than a single religion.

"Also of note is the fact that there are several gods in Hinduism. I will give you a few examples:

"Brahma, the Creator…

"Vishnu, the Preserver…

"Shiva, the Destroyer…

"Ganapati, the Remover of Obstacles…

"Saraswati, the Goddess of Learning…

"That in a nutshell is what Hinduism is all about.

"I will now hand over to *Professor* Anitha to give you a brief insight into the reasons why Hindus generally do not consume beef!"

"Why do you call me Professor?" Anitha laughed.

"Kakra, you have to respect her – a very brilliant young lady", Sunitha said. "I am also gifted, but she is more ambitious than me. Indeed, if our parents had had the means to further our education we would be very high on the academic ladder."

"I don't want to pass any comment on that", Anitha smiled, "so here we go with my presentation:

"The cow remains a protected animal in Hinduism, revered as a symbol of life and may never be killed; indeed, the overwhelming majority of Hindus do not eat beef.

"Many streams of the Hinduism consider the cow a motherly god, a gentle spirit who is often treated as a member of the family.

"You yourself pointed out that you were surprised to see them roaming the streets. Due to their protected status they really abound in India. Many visitors to India are surprised at the number of cows that roam the streets unhindered.

"Most rural Indian families have at least one dairy cow. The milk of the family cow nourishes children as they grow up. Indeed, when for whatever reasons a baby cannot be breastfed by the mother, the cow is prescribed as the choice of surrogate breast feeding.

"The cow dung (*gobar*) is a major source of energy for households throughout India. Indeed most Indians do not share the revulsion that others have for cow excrement, but instead consider it an earthy and useful natural product.

"The five products (*pancagavya*) of the cow – milk, curds, ghee butter, urine and dung – are all used in *puja* (worship) as well as in rites of extreme penance.

"Once a year the cow is honoured, on *Gopastami*, what has become known as 'Cow Holiday'. On such occasions, cows are washed and decorated in the temple and given offerings in the hope that her gifts of life will continue.

"Now we have given you some broad knowledge of our culture and religion.

"It is now you turn to answer a question that has been burning on my mind since our first meeting. I do not know whether Anitha has any questions for you. My question is:

"Why is your country called the Gold Coast?"

"Well, it has also been on my mind to ask you ladies why you Indian women seem to be fascinated with gold. Indeed, right from the time of our arrival here, I have observed women on the streets wearing necklaces, bracelets, ear rings, etc., all of gold.

"On one occasion, during a trip to town with one of our Indian mates, he took us to a wedding involving a relative. I just could not imagine it – but the bride wore so many different gold necklaces around her slim neck that for a while I thought it was going to break!

"Of course, we wanted to find out why she couldn't do with less. Our mate couldn't provide any convincing answer. Never mind, I'll leave the question open for now and give you a lecture on the Gold Coast. I will return to you later for an answer to my question.

"On the matter of the Gold Coast, I'll provide you with only a brief account.

"The answer is simple: On their arrival in the Gold Coast, the first thing the first Europeans saw was the gold along the shores of the coast... 'Gold!' they shouted at the top of their voices, 'Gold as far as the eye could see!'

"And so they called the coast the Gold Coast. But we are talking about the whole country, not just the coast, of course. Though the colony changed hands between Europeans – the Portuguese to the Danes and finally to the English – the name 'Gold Coast' has been maintained.

"I am not aware as to how much gold was moved out of the Gold Coast to adorn the palaces of various European Kings and Queens since the first Europeans, the Portuguese, first set their feet on the Gold Coast in 1471, right up to this day in 1946 that I am speaking to you, but the amount without doubt was massive, really massive!"

"Do you think there is still something left for Anitha and myself?" Sunitha smiled.

"Definitely, definitely", Kakra laughed. "I am from the Asante territory of the Gold Coast, and the unifying symbol of the Asante kingdom is a Golden Stool, or Golden Throne, a heavy seat made of pure gold that is purported to have descended from the skies."

"Descended from the skies?" Sunitha inquired with a degree of scepticism written on her face.

"A myth or reality?" Anitha added her voice.

"Well, my dear friends, it is said to have come down from the clear blue skies on a sunny day! It is said to have happened around 1700; even my great, great grandfather was not born at that time. There are no written eyewitness accounts of that spectacular occurrence – only oral tradition. One may either choose to accept it as a fact or…."

"Or discard it – and that is what I will do!" Sunitha interrupted him.

"Anyway, that is only an aside in the matter of – the fact remains that the Gold Coast, in particular its Asante region, abounds in gold."

"Kakra, can you believe it!" Sunitha exclaimed.

"What?"

"I just began to daydream, daydream of a time when I will be wearing jewellery made of Asante gold – necklaces, earrings, wrist bracelets, etc. – in a fairy tale wedding!"

"Any idea of your bridegroom's identity?" her sister asked sarcastically.

"I was fancying a fairy-tale prince, but his face was obscure!"

"Kakra, perhaps?" Anitha pressed her.

"No, not me!" Kakra exclaimed. "I wouldn't know how to handle such an attractive Indian princess!"

"I can coach you in the matter."

"Well, let's see what the future has in store for all of us. I have now finished my brief discourse into the matter of Gold Coast gold. Now you have to explain why Indian women seem to be obsessed with gold!"

"Well, I will volunteer for the task", Anitha smiled. "Briefly it is for the following reasons:

"Firstly, gold is considered a status symbol; indeed, a symbol of wealth. I don't consider that as a typical Indian trait but rather as a universal phenomenon. I don't know the situation in the Gold Coast, but surely it is true of many other societies.

"It is in regard to what I am about to say that Indians may differ from others. In India, gold worn by a bride in a wedding ceremony shows her family's status and wealth. Besides that, it is generally held that luck and happiness will forever be the lot of the bride who wears 24-carat gold jewellery on their wedding day."

After interacting for a while, they decided to bring the meeting to an end, to give each party sufficient time to catch their respective trains. Before parting company, they agreed to meet around noon at their usual meeting point exactly a week from that day.

As he lay in bed that night Kakra began to think about his meeting with the splendid Indian twins. Was he falling in love with them? If that was the case, with which of the two? As far as their appearance was concerned, he had already established that there was nothing to tell them apart.

Yet, there was something Anitha possessed, something which though he was unable to formulate in words, seemed to make him feel marginally more attracted to her than to Sunitha!

* * *

Two days after his meeting with his new-found Indian friends, Kakra's unit was told to get ready to board a ship that was due to dock at their port of departure in ten days' time. The news was met with a rapturous outburst of joy by Kakra and his mates. At long last, almost five months to the day when the first batch from the 81st Division left for home, it was their turn to do the same.

Much as he was overjoyed at the prospect of seeing not only his family, but also his native land, the idea of leaving his new-found friends behind cast a shadow on his joy.

He turned up for the meeting with them as planned. On this occasion, his friends decided to take him on a walk around the little town, to show him interesting places including their respective schools.

As they strolled along the streets of the town, the conversation centred first on their respective families. They were the first to request Kakra to tell them about his family background.

Next, they gave him a brief account of their backgrounds. They were part of the majority Hindi-speaking population. As they had already mentioned on the previous occasion, they ascribed to the Hindu religion. They had five other siblings – a brother who was three years their senior, three younger sisters as well as a younger brother.

After strolling around for a while, Kakra decided to let the cat out of the bag.

"It's a pity we did not meet at the very beginning of my stay in the South East; "unfortunately, this is going to be our last meeting!" he declared.

"No, for God's sake, no!" Sunitha exclaimed.

"What's the matter – are we getting on your nerves?" Anitha inquired.

"Not at all! I have enjoyed your company. You are really amazing individuals. As I mentioned the other time, we have virtually been sitting on packed luggage since the end of the campaign in Burma, which feels like ages. The first batch of the Gold Coast troops left here a few months ago. Well, it is now my turn to do the same."

"So, when are you leaving?" Anitha inquired, barely able to hold back her tears.

"On Wednesday."

"This coming Wednesday?"

"Yes."

"That's a shame, a real shame!"

A short silence was broken by Anitha.

"Is it possible to meet again? If even for a short time? I want to give you a present – something that hopefully will not only place joy in your heart, but also serve as a reminder of your time with the talkative Indian twins!"

"Yes, I can make it. I have already packed all my items – I have some time at my disposal."

"Then let's meet on Tuesday afternoon, at our usual meeting spot at the railway station."

With heavy heart Kakra parted company with his awesome Indian friends and returned to the military base.

At the appointed time, Sunitha and Anitha turned up for the meeting. Accompanying them was a teenage boy who they introduced as their 15-year-old junior brother Rajiv. He was fascinated with Africa, Sunitha revealed, and was desirous of visiting their uncle in Kampala. He had hoped to meet Kakra on a possible visit to their homes but since that was no longer possible he had decided to come to say hello and at the same time bid him farewell.

As a farewell gift, the twins gave him pictures of themselves – depicting each of them alone and then together.

On his part, he presented them with a picture of himself taken a few weeks before. Taking pictures of himself on his furloughs to town had become one of the favourite pastimes. Initially he had made a joke of his "bush" African friends who seemed to be fascinated with the technology behind photography and took advantage of every excursion to town to call on the next available photo shop to take pictures. He had in the meantime made the habit his own.

After interacting with each other for a while, the time came for them to bid a final farewell. With tears flowing freely from their eyes, each of the two sisters took turns to embrace their friend from Africa in an emotional farewell.

Kakra, who hardly showed emotions, was so moved that he could hardly hold back his tears.

Finally, the train to take him back to the barracks pulled up at the station. Giving each of the three siblings a final hug, he climbed onto the train.

As the train pulled out of the station, he kept his gaze fixed on his friends, until they finally faded out of sight.

Chapter 49
Daydreaming of imminent liberation during a long ocean crossing

—*mm*—

A S PLANNED, Kakra and his mates boarded a special train arranged for the troops whose turn it was to depart for home the next morning and headed for Madras.

At long last they were putting the isolated camp behind them. As they journeyed on, Kakra could hardly wait for the day when he would finally set foot on the Gold Coast.

After about three hours' ride on the train, the train pulled to a stop at a station a few hundred metres from the port of Madras. From there the troops marched to board their troopship.

With the Mediterranean and the Suez Canal safe from Nazi threat, they were told the return journey would be along that route instead of around the Cape of Good Hope, which they had taken on the journey to India about two years before.

As he sat on the deck of the ship, his gaze fixed on the water mass that seemed to be boundless, he looked forward eagerly to a reunion with his family; his only prayer was that, unlike the period following his return from East Africa, nothing unforeseeable would set in to prevent that from happening.

One thing he was very certain of, and indeed he was absolutely convinced of it – there would be no unforeseeable circumstances that would result in he and his mates from the Empire being called upon to head for yet another battlefield – no, not within the borders of the Gold

Coast, not within the borders of Africa, and indeed not in the whole wide world!

Why was he so certain of this? As they waited, he had occupied himself with both listening to the news on the radio and watching it on TV. The impression made on him was that Britain was itself grappling with the aftermath of the disastrous events of the worldwide war that had just come to an end. The task of repairing and rebuilding the British Isles following the devastations brought about by the war was Herculean, to say the least. In such a scenario, who would think the policy makers would have the appetite to engage in any further military conflicts in the very near future?

He also had plenty of time to reflect on his almost seven years in the army. Among other things, the army had exposed him to different parts of the world, different cultures, different kinds of foods, different kinds of dressing, a new range of ideas, etc. It has also given him the opportunity to interact with people of different backgrounds. Prior to his abduction he had not travelled far; indeed, the farthest he had travelled was to Kofikrom, the district capital. Apart from the few Ewes who had settled in Kojokrom to engage in farming, he had had no contact with any different ethnic group of the colony apart from members of his own Akan ethnicity.

His time in the army had offered him the opportunity to get to know other members of different ethnic groups of the colony – Dagombas, Gas, Hausas, Krobos, Nzemas, etc. Beyond that, by virtue of his tour of duty in both East Africa and Burma, he had come across additional population groups – Yorubas, Igbos, Madingos, Indians, Poles, English etc. Talking of the English, the British! He had by virtue of the war the opportunity to interact with the British, his colonial masters, as it were. Previously he had regarded them as a kind of super human being – no longer! Serving with them on the battlefield, he had seen them thirsty, hungry, scared, running for their lives, shot at, injured and killed!

If there was anything that he counted worthy of the hardships, misery, pain, hassle, etc., that he had to endure over the time, it was the realisation that there was no point in the Gold Coast and other countries in Africa and elsewhere under colonial rule to remain so in the foreseeable future. Indeed, he was determined to do whatever he could to ensure independence from colonial rule happened as soon as possible.

The reader can be spared a detailed account of Kakra's return journey, which proved to be uneventful.

Chapter 50
Home again, home again!

~~~

THE TROOPSHIP carrying Kakra berthed at the port of Takoradi in the middle of August 1946. Relatives of some of the servicemen, especially those in urban centres with access to radio, print media and other sources of information, had received word of the return of the war heroes and had gathered to welcome their loved ones.

The Takoradi municipal council on its part had organised a brass band ensemble to play patriotic songs to bid the patriotic combatants "Welcome Home!"

After disembarking from the ship, Kakra and his fellow soldiers were transported by trucks to the Takoradi military base, into a temporary accommodation facility especially prepared for the war returnees.

In contrast to the time of his departure, there was virtually no foreign military presence at either the seaport or the airport.

"Everyone has left; Takoradi has served its purpose", he was told by a soldier of the base he had engaged in conversation in the course of his stay.

"No commemorative memorial then, in the city or elsewhere, in honour of the men, both dead and alive, who had played various roles?" he asked, dismayed. "No recalling how they had assembled the planes, servicing the aircrafts and ships, braving the hazardous route to fly long distances to supply troops in North Africa, to ensure victory for King and Empire?"

"Maybe those who have the last word are considering the matter."

"Or maybe a positive decision has already been taken and the corresponding structure is being designed or even being built at a factory somewhere?"

"Well, let's hope so. As you can see for yourself, however, nothing has been installed here yet."

"I hope they don't forget your vital role, my dear Takoradi!" Kakra stated.

"Well, you and I can only conjecture!"

* * *

After spending about three weeks in the "acclimatisation centre", the order finally came for Kakra and other servicemen who hailed from Asante and the regions to the north of it, to get ready to leave the base the next day.

Prior to their departure each soldier was paid a gratuity for services to the Empire. The amount involved was not uniform and depended on the length of service. Kakra was paid £35, which almost amounted to a fortune in those days.

As he would soon realise, however, it did not possess the same purchasing power as compared to the time when he departed the shores of the Gold Coast for his tour of duty to Burma three years before.

The war had not only led to the separation of loved ones, as in the case of Kakra and several thousands of Gold Coast service personnel who served on the battlefield, but also had a negative impact on the economy, leading to significant price increases.

After taking almost a day, the northbound train finally pulled to a stop at the central train station of Kumasi just before the fall of darkness.

That was the first time in his life that he set foot on the soil of the Asante capital.

Much as he had wished to visit the Asante metropolis during the time he was growing up in Kojokrom, he never had the opportunity to do so until the events the reader is already familiar with.

Several military trucks, sent to pick up the men, lined up in a large open court overlooking the station. Apart from the vehicles, a handful of soldiers were there to help them pack their items and belongings onto the trucks. About 15 minutes after their arrival, the convoy of military trucks set out on the journey to the military barracks, about 15 minutes' drive away.

After spending a few days there, Kakra with several others were finally handed their demobilisation papers, thereby ending his almost seven years' engagement with the army.

Though forced into it through circumstances beyond his control, an emotional bond had in the meantime developed between Kakra and the military. The soldiery existence had become part of his existence; the raw daily regimented routine had become part and parcel of his life.

Chapter 51
A tumultuous welcome for a *dead man walking*

~~~~

E arly in the morning, which heralded the day of their discharge from the army, the fresh ex-servicemen were driven in military trucks to Kejetia, a suburb of Kumasi and dropped at the central lorry station where they would board a vehicle for their respective destinations.

Kakra was of course more than eager to get home. For a while he considered hiring a taxi to take him home as quickly as possible instead of waiting for a normal passenger vehicle, which was likely to stop at almost every town on the way to allow passengers to either disembark or embark or both, adding to the journey time. On second thoughts, however, he decided to abandon the idea. The main reason was financial. As mentioned earlier, he was paid a gratuity of £35 for his military service. Though it amounted to a fortune at that time, he did not lose sight of the fact that it was a one-off payment.

Though he had resisted the army from day one of his conscription, it offered a steady monthly income. With his discharge from the military he could no longer rely on that steady income. He resolved therefore to hold on tenaciously to the gratuity payment and not give it out unnecessarily.

A large Bedford passenger truck was the first in line. As was usual with such trucks, it had two cabins. The front cabin was small and built with metal. It offered room for three persons, the driver and two others. The second cabin could be described as a huge wooden cage. Within it, arranged in rows of about seven, were long wooden seats. Each row offered seating for five passengers. After waiting patiently for about an hour for the truck to fill up, the driver finally set it in motion. It was his policy that every available space was filled before departure.

Midway through the journey, it began to rain; initially it was a drizzle, which later became a torrential downpour. After about an hour they reached Oseikrom. It was still raining but not as heavily as before.

His heart began to beat faster and faster, the closer he neared his place of birth. In due course, the excitement building up in him was almost unbearable. How would the little town react to his sudden return? Had they in the meantime got word of Nyamekye's passing away in East Africa? If they hadn't, how should he go about breaking the tragic news to his family? Should he do it on the very first day of his return or wait a few days?

The driver had made it clear to Kakra at the outset that his intended final destination was Oseikrom. He would only consider taking the trouble to continue on to Kojokrom if there were at least five passengers in the little community as their final destination – which to the delight of Kakra turned out to be the case.

As the driver set his vehicle in motion on the last leg of Kakra's journey home from Burma, Kakra wondered which of his co-passengers were heading for Kojokrom, for none of them looked familiar to him. Were they strangers visiting the village – perhaps for the first time? Or were they individuals who had moved to settle in his beloved hometown during his absence?

Whatever their connections to the village, he was glad they were unfamiliar to him. He knew the nature and mentality of his people. Had there been any residents of the village familiar with him and his case in the vehicle, the joy and excitement of seeing him after so many years' absence would have led the person or persons to have created such a scene that it would have drawn the attention of those far and near to them! He was not in the mood to become involved in any such hullabaloo, certainly not in the centre of the Asante metropolis.

The stop at Oseikrom turned out to be longer than anticipated. Just as the driver was about to take off to head for Kojokrom, someone drew his attention to the fact that one of the back tyres appeared to be partially deflated. The driver got down to check it.

"Damn it, the second-hand tyre dealer has given me a raw deal!" he lamented. "Never mind, next time I will be careful."

Fortunately, he happened to have a pump in the vehicle. With it, his assistant got to work to inflate the tyre.

"He just needs to put in sufficient air to get us to Kojokrom", the driver explained to his passengers. "I will change the tyre when we get there." One of his passengers was becoming ever more impatient than Kakra about the delay.

Kakra thought there would be no more delays thereafter, but as it turned out his patience would be tested further.

"I am running low on fuel", the driver said. "I didn't have enough money to buy a full tank. I need to top up a bit, otherwise we could get stuck on the way."

"My goodness", Kakra murmured under his breath, "I should perhaps have taken the taxi after all!"

Finally, the driver set his vehicle in motion. After about half an hour's drive, just as they were about half a mile from the outskirts of Kojokrom, Kakra, who was deeply absorbed in thoughts about his imminent reunion with his family in particular, and the community at large, spotted two individuals, male and female, just about his age, walking along the roadside carrying loads on their heads and heading in the same direction as themselves.

Just as the vehicle drove past them, he took a closer look at the pair. Then he recognised him – Panin, his brother!

"Panina, Panin!" he shouted spontaneously and began to wave.

The noise from the engine, coupled with that of the rain, smothered his voice.

If only he could talk to the driver to urge him to pull his vehicle to a stop – but no, he couldn't. As already pointed out, the driver sat in a metal enclosure with only a small glass window between them, but it was shut.

Kakra wished he could spring out of the vehicle and head back to his brother!

He waved and waved.

"Do you know him?" one of those travelling with him inquired.

"Yes indeed!" he replied without going into any further details.

Kakra wished the vehicle could take wings and fly the remaining distance, to permit him to get down and rush back where they came from to meet his beloved brother!

Finally, after driving about five minutes along the rugged and bumpy road, the vehicle, at Kakra's request, pulled to a stop just near the extended family home.

As he stepped out of the vehicle, Kakra's sister Tawiah, who happened to be returning home from a visit to a friend, and who was shielded from the drizzling rain by an umbrella, turned casually to look at the vehicle that had just made a stop not far from their home.

As she did so she noticed that the gentleman disembarking bore a close resemblance to Panin. That Panin had left for the farm with Henewaah was no secret to her. Since one had to walk about half a mile along the road before joining a bush path leading to the farm, she initially thought the driver had been kind to them and offered them a lift to save them from having to walk the distance through the rain.

But the gentleman who had in the meantime got down from the vehicle and was in the process of removing his luggage was not wearing "bush wear" – the term the residents had coined to describe clothes worn for work on the farm; so, she surmised, it could not be Panin.

In the meantime, Kakra had recognised his favourite sister!

"Akosua Tawiah!" he yelled at the top of his voice.

Her thoughts were so focussed on Panin that she never thought it could be Kakra. How could she – after all those years of his absence, with absolutely no sign of life coming from his end?

Could it indeed be Kakra?

For a moment, she thought she was daydreaming.

"Akosua Tawiah, my dear younger sister, it is *me*, your brother Kakra, back from captivity!"

"Kofi Kakra! Is that you indeed, or your ghost?" she exclaimed and dashed towards him.

"If you believe in ghosts then you are seeing the GHOST of your 'dead' brother; otherwise you are seeing him in flesh and blood!"

In the meantime, she had caught up with him. With outstretched arms she embraced her dear brother crying aloud his name, so loud it was heard at a considerable distance away. At the same time neither of them could control their tears, as they flowed freely.

Meanwhile Adwoa Achiaa, Tawaih's six-year-old daughter, who had heard the case of her missing uncle several times over since the time she was big enough to understand, ran to the extended family home to spread the news.

"Uncle Kakra is here, Uncle Kakra is back, Uncle Kakra!" she shouted at the top of her voice.

"Don't try to make fun of us; it is a serious matter", Asoh cautioned her.

"I swear by Almighty God, it is true!"

"Hey little girl, you don't have to swear to God", Duku cautioned her. "Now come here. Look into my eyes and repeat what you are saying if indeed that is true."

"Yes, it is really true, Kakra is back!"

At that stage, everyone at home rushed outside to have a look. Asoh was so overcome with joy she nearly collapsed to the floor when she attempted to join the group.

"Duku, help me; I do not feel stable on my legs."

"Someone spread a mat for her to rest on."

Soon the instruction was followed. After lying on the mat for a while she regained strength.

Meanwhile, Kakra had freed himself from the entanglement of his younger sister, who seemed to want to cling to him indefinitely as if in an attempt to prevent any future abduction, and was heading in the direction the vehicle had come from.

"Where are you heading for?" Tawiah inquired.

"To Panin."

"But he is at work on the farm."

"No, he is on his way home. We drove past him, a woman walking beside him. Is he married?"

"Yes indeed, his wife is Henewaah."

Kakra's brisk walking had in the meantime turned into running. He was followed by a large part of the children and the youth of the village who had poured onto the streets at the news of his arrival.

Soon he caught sight of Panin in the distance.

At that juncture, he began to wave both hands in the air, shouting as he ran: "Panin, I am back! Panin, I am back! Panin, it is me – Kakra; I am back!"

Panin immediately recognised the distinctive voice of his brother, his soulmate – the voice that was indistinguishable from that of his own, and was soon rushing towards him.

Instantly he tossed the firewood he was carrying on his head into the air. Henewaah had to spring quickly aside to avoid being hit by the wood that rebounded and flew in all directions.

"Kakra, my dear!"

Panin shouted at the top of his voice and sprang forward, running as fast as his legs could carry him.

At just about the same speed Kakra also raced towards his brother.

They might have wished to break the sound barrier! As it turned out, neither of them could brake sufficiently to prevent a collision! Moments later both went crashing to the bare ground but felt no pain – for what was pain in their highly charged emotional state?

For the next few minutes both, firmly entangled in an embrace, rolled and rolled, indeed kept rolling on the bare earth, in the process completely soiling their clothes with mud and dirt!

"Kakra? Or his ghost?" exclaimed Panin.

"The real Kakra!"

"Sure?"

"Sure, sure!"

"Today, even if I die today, I won't be bothered!"

"Hey Panin, don't say that; who will take care of your children when you are gone?"

"Kakra!"

"But I also need you, Panin!" Kakra yelled at the top of his voice.

Meanwhile both had risen to their feet. Still entangled in each other, they hopped and jumped around for a while.

It was a real spectacle to behold!

The news of Kakra's return spread through the little settlement like wildfire. The happy event virtually turned the whole community upside down. It had in the meantime stopped raining. Though the streets had turned muddy and slippery following the downpour, no one seemed to care and braved the hazard and came out to witness the return of the *lost son,* as many of them put it. Soon, almost every inhabitant of the little town, boasting a population of about a thousand, was on the street.

At the extended family home, everyone, from the smallest child old enough to appreciate the occasion to the oldest of the very elderly, was plunged into a state of frenzied jubilation on the return of Kakra.

Asoh, Duku and the direct siblings of the twins – Tawiah, Nyankomagoh, Kofi Anane, Adwoa Anum, Kwaku Nsiah, Nana Yaw and Akosua Kaakyire – seemed for a while to be intoxicated with joy at the sudden and unannounced return of Kakra.

In due course Kakra was introduced to some of the new members of the family, his sister-in-law Henewaah as well as their two little children, six-year-old Kakra Junior (named after Kakra) and four-year-old Nana Duku (named after their father). Not to be forgotten in the family roll call was Asoh's last child, four-year-old Akosua Kaakyire. Kakra was especially delighted to see his pretty little sister.

Kakra's return was not only greeted with explosions of emotions of joy from his family members but from residents of Kojokrom as a whole.

For a while, the outpouring of emotion seemed to have no end, a situation that eventually led him to resolve to stay at home for a while; such was the number of people who thronged around him to shake his hand, hug him, all eager to inquire about his war experiences whenever he ventured outside, that he took refuge indoors, the pressure for his attention having become too much to bear.

As regards Nyamekye, Kakra had all along thought his relatives had already formally been informed by the army about his demise in the East African campaign. However, as it turned out, due to an error in the initial registration process, his place of birth was indicated as Kojokrom in the Fanti area instead of Asante. As Kakra later found out, the military turned up at Fanti-Kojokrom about 170 kilometres from their town, only to be told he was unknown in the area. Perhaps as a result of the pressure on the military to prepare for yet another foreign engagement in Burma, no further effort was made to trace his roots.

On the day following his return, Kakra was resting at home when Nyamekye's parents called on him to inquire about his whereabouts.

Kakra had the difficult task, not only of breaking the sad news of their son's death to them, but also to inform them, as far as he was aware, that his body could not be retrieved from the battlefield.

The only consolation he could offer them was to bring the matter to the attention of the military with the goal of securing the entitlement due to him for his relatives.

The news of the tragic end of Nyamekye spread quickly into the community to cast a shadow on the otherwise euphoric mood of jubilation that had prevailed since Kakra's return.

EPILOGUE
Joys and challenges of liberation

⟶ππ⟵

INITIALLY Kakra was indecisive as to the way forward – whether to settle in the little village or move to a bigger place such as Kumasi, Accra, Takoradi, Cape Coast, etc.

After wrestling with himself for a while as to what to do next, he finally resolved to establish himself at his place of birth. He decided to invest part of his military entitlement in farming, part in the setting up of a pub, while keeping the remainder in the bank.

For a while after his return, he yearned for the company of Sunitha and Anitha. With not only a huge water mass, both the Indian and Atlantic oceans separating them, but also insufficient means at his disposal to finance a voyage to visit them or arrange for them to tour the Gold Coast, he would at best have to limit communication to letters. Even then he had to abandon that idea, for there was still neither a post office at Kojokrom, nor had the community hired a letterbox at Oseikrom.

"Agitate for the independence of your respective countries on your return", Jack the African had urged them. Even without taking the advice of his dear English friend into consideration, his wartime experience had, as far as he was concerned, made living under colonial rule a non-starter.

While yearning for the privilege of living in an independent country, if only for the time being, he had to come to terms with the status quo – a fact that he found quite difficult to swallow.

His indignation towards colonial rule was inflamed further by the events of February 28, 1948. On that occasion, a peaceful demonstration by ex-servicemen was violently broken up by the police, leaving three ex-servicemen dead.

Eventually he joined the Convention People's Party (CPP) and helped galvanise support for independence in his locality. Curiously Panin, while not against independence *per se*, advocated for a gradual approach to self-rule.

Eventually the Gold Coast gained independence on March 6, 1957, and was renamed Ghana.

A detailed account of how the two brothers followed the independence struggle in the Gold Coast and developments in post-independent Ghana from their respective perspectives is set out in the book, *Twins Divided*.

www.ingramcontent.com/pod-product-compliance
Lightning Source LLC
LaVergne TN
LVHW051507080426
835509LV00017B/1952